ROSY COLE

A House Not Made With Hands

A novelised history of a celebrated Wreake Valley chapel

First published by New Eve Publishing 2024

Copyright © 2024 by Rosy Cole

All rights reserved. No part of this publication may be reproduced, stored or transmitted in any form or by any means, electronic, mechanical, photocopying, recording, scanning, or otherwise without written permission from the publisher. It is illegal to copy this book, post it to a website, or distribute it by any other means without permission.

Rosy Cole asserts the moral right to be identified as the author of this work.

Third edition

ISBN: 978-1-7399801-3-9

New Eve Publishing
Great Britain

In loving memory of Una Jordan and all those faithful pilgrims who lit my path

Contents

Foreword	ii
1 The Fallow Land	1
2 The Ploughed Field	3
3 The Sown Seed	32
4 The Wheat and The Tares	62
5 The Harvest	78
6 The New Grain	108
7 The New Crop?	121

Foreword

I hope readers will enjoy this novella more than a dry chronicle of events and will forgive the liberty of a 'fictional' reconstruction.

Grateful thanks to Ray Young and Frances Lewis for the loan of books and documents and the Revd Martin Smithson for his informative letters.

RJC

1

The Fallow Land

1745

On Moody Bush Hill, just off the bridle path which traces a lackadaisical course to South Croxton, stands a forgotten relic of feudal times. It is neither milestone nor monolith, neither cairn nor cornerstone, a granite tooth inscribed with the words *Moody Bush*. No one knows how it came to be there or who was the mason who tooled its weather-hewn face. Legend claims that it marks the meeting place of the old hundreds court which debated local affairs when William the Conqueror took it into his head that the Gallic touch was needed to civilise the mongrel peasants of this island. Where the mighty emperors of Rome had failed, he would not!

It is an idyllic landscape, thickly populated with oak and ash, with elder, blackthorn and sycamore, diligently tilled for almost a thousand years since the Vikings first tamed its forests and subdued its stubborn clay with their peerless ploughshares. It rests at the heart of a heart-shaped county, about as far from any alien horizon or the cut and thrust of everything associated with seafaring as you can get.

Queniborough nestles in the valley, distinguished by the dragon's tail spire of St. Mary's church, and a mile or two to the north-west, the tower of St. Peter's Church rises foursquare in the parish of Syston. In the archaic tongue of its Anglo-Saxon settlers, the tiny hamlet was named Sithestun after the broad, blunt stone where its patriarchs gathered.

Little affects the tempo of its days. The warring factions to the north and south which contest the right of the Catholic Stuart over the Protestant Hanoverian for the nation's throne are no more than a whispered rumour. Ever since the Roman occupation, shiresfolk have preferred to cherish their roots rather than tangle with offcomers. The fact that St. Augustine, despatched by Pope Gregory I to these pagan shores, had converted Offa, descendant of Eowa, King Penda of Mercia's brother, and the kingdom had grown fat and prosperous as a result, has long passed from memory. Those who work the land assume God's in his heaven and that they know how life should be lived.

But deep below their pattens and hunting-boots, nature still seethes. The middle ground is riven by an ancient fault line. Some say that, until the titanic upheavals of the Ice Age, the undulating plain which forms the backbone of Charnwood Forest was the highest range of peaks in England. Every so often the earth's core rumbles and sends forth a shuddering ripple which undermines buildings, causes lightning cracks to appear in plasterwork and stirs up a gale. Thunderstorms occur more regularly than anywhere else in the British Isles.

Today, these rocky outcrops, Breedon Hill, Beacon Hill, Burrough Hill, fortresses from the cradle of man, are stations in a chain of beacons. They might warn of advancing armies, hail a new sovereign or proclaim the birth of his heir.

So much for earthquake, wind and fire. But what of the still, small voice…?

2

The Ploughed Field

1745

"Ah, Leicestershire," sighed John Wesley as his mount kicked over a stony track, "where I always feel such liberty and see but little fruit!"

He had just taken his leave of the brethren at Markfield, the foothold of his ministry in the Charnwood Forest, when a flushed and breathless rider came galloping alongside. At once he recognised John Coltman, a hosier from Leicester with whom he had dined on several occasions. Not long ago the poor fellow had been gravely depressed and had tried all manner of remedies until the little preacher had laid hands on him and called down the blessing of the Heavenly Physician.

"Mr Wesley, sir, I heard tell you were abroad in these parts. Won't you come and speak to the good folk of the town?"

Wesley reached out and put a lightly consoling hand beneath his companion's elbow. "I don't wilfully neglect them, my friend. I must go where I'm most needed and the Spirit leads elsewhere. There's a deal of trouble brewing in the Border Country since Charles Edward Stuart landed on these shores."

"Ay, he'll do away wi' King George and turn us all into Papists!"

"He's a long way to go before that, thank God. But we must not underestimate the strength of Jacobite feeling. Tis an odd irony that we

Methodists, as Dissenters from the Established Church, are oftentimes mistaken for Catholics. Our sect is everywhere spoken against."

"Then they suffer much in the North?"

"Praise God, they do!" beamed the wiry clergyman. "There's nothing to make the gospel thrive so much as persecution. The best Christians are to be found among the strongholds of the devil. Go and tell them in the town to pray for a happy outcome of these affairs and I engage to visit you on my return."

The comrades parted, the hosier to broadcast this heartening exchange, the man of God to reflect on the phlegmatic nature of these Midlanders. Many was the time he had passed through the county and expounded the faith in its villages, but the area did not beckon strongly enough and the town scarcely at all. They were peaceable folk, he knew, spinners and weavers whose grinding toil had brought a fair degree of economic stability to the region. Sometimes they would rise in the small hours, walking miles out of their way to hear his message before work began, but though they listened with interest, they were slow to respond. Materialism was their god and guide and they thought nothing of plundering every wagon that entered the town gates to sell its goods at inflated prices.

If only they could raise their heads above their wheels and treadles and glimpse eternity.

****

"Plough a straight furrow, lad," William's father would counsel. "Fix your eye on the far side and never look back."

The cultivation of crops and the tending of beasts ran in George Cooper's blood. Both his own and his wife's families had been farmers for generations so that William could not fail to possess an easy affinity with the land.

William loved the rolling Wreake Valley with its winding watercourses, lush meadows and plains where sheep might safely graze. On his return from Melton Mowbray market, footsore and weary from goading the stock, he would marvel at the curious transparency of the air around Rotherby whose cottages snuggled under the square-towered church like chicks about a mother hen. His mother had been Hannah Fletcher, a Syston maid born and bred, whom her husband had carried off to Rotherby after their wedding on All Fool's Day, 1746. It had long been a joke that George had put his head in the noose on so inauspicious a day! That very month, news had reached them of the Jacobite defeat at Culloden in the Scottish Highlands. Bonnie Prince Charlie's hopes of the Crown had been dashed. The Hanoverian redcoats had butchered the Stuart forces and gone far beyond the call of duty in laying waste the Gaelic way of life. Having next to no idea what they were fighting for, half of them, they had sorely punished the brazen-faced clansmen, but the Prince had cunningly slipped through their fingers and gone scuttling back to France. It seemed that Protestant and Catholic had been forever at each other's throats and William, who was given to pondering these matters, was at a loss to fathom why those who proclaimed one Lord could not live in reasonable harmony.

By now, the third George in succession was on the throne. He was German, of course, but unlike his predecessors, spoke English as well as any Charterhouse schoolmaster. He distrusted the nobility for their ambiguous values and preferred to consort with simple mortals. Farming fascinated him. He had a model farm at Kew for the instruction of the young Princes in his overflowing nursery. When he went to take the air at Weymouth, he loved to linger over a breakfast of boiled ham and oatcakes in the kitchen of some local farmhouse while he and the overawed tenant mulled over the problems of good husbandry.

The trouble was that the old ways were changing fast. New techniques were being pioneered to make the growing of the nation's food more efficient. Over in Norfolk, Viscount Coke insisted on the importance of crop rotation. Did he imagine that cottagers could afford to let their strips lie fallow for one year in three? To cap it all, landowners were looking for new means of fattening their pockets. They preferred to see their affairs managed by a dozen large tenants than chase scraps of rent from scores of small ones. This meant that country people were having to turn to labouring and were losing a pride in tending their own patch. Everywhere, land was being enclosed by hawthorn hedges which cost good money to maintain and left little common where you could scratch out a living with a pig or a cow. Fodder had to be begged, bought or stolen.

William was used to hearing his parents discuss these things long into the night over a guttering tallow candle. They had had their share of hardships but had well survived. "Make no mistake, Will, the Lord always provides," his mother would declare, "though not without a vast deal of toiling and spinning from me!"

"How can you be sure?" he had probed as a youngster, though he entertained less doubt of her than of the Almighty.

She was pummelling dough at the time, her freckled brown arms powdered with flour. "Do I take bricks out of the oven when I bake a loaf? See this! Left in the warm for a couple of hours, twill be twice the size and more full of hot air than the vicar!" Hers was a mischievous heresy. While she had the deepest respect for the tenets of the Christian religion, a lively nature occasionally drove her to poke fun at the Church as an ecclesiastical institution.

"Is it magic, then?" asked her son, turning his bright face up to her.

"Little nippers ask too many questions and that's a fact."

"But is it?"

"Well, maybe it is and maybe it isn't. You might call yeast magic in a manner o' speaking. Tis like faith, like saying your prayers and believing you'll receive what you need."

Now that he had reached the age of twenty, William's contribution to the rent was substantial. He was a broad-shouldered youth of medium height with a mop of yellow hair tied back with twine, a skilful farmer with a propensity for book-learning. Before he was three, he had mastered the alphabet from a hornbook at his mother's knee and a year later was composing whole sentences upon his slate.

"Give over stuffing the boy's head with these clever notions," George Cooper cautioned. "It'll do naught to put bread on the table."

But Hannah thought she knew better. If God had given her son talents, he would not readily see them squandered.

That spring, on his weekly expeditions to market, William fell in with

THE PLOUGHED FIELD

a lively crowd from Frisby-on-the-Wreake and they began discussing the Methodist travelling preachers who had recently visited the village.

"They're naught but rabble, those tub-thumpers," sneered one fellow. "They've no place in church and no place out of it."

"Nay, lad," replied the shepherd among them, "there are them as go to the meetings to make trouble and them as go to listen."

"Damnable barngoers, the vicar calls 'em," piped up the goatherd. "He's no time for 'em, that's for sure."

"Old Wragge's no time for anyone who can't invite him to table," grumbled the burly stockman, "unless you've an itch to be matched in a hurry without licence or banns. He does a fine trade in that!"

"Tis my belief," owned the shepherd boldly, "there's summat in what them gospellers say. Sam Letts is a changed man since he heard the Call. He don't rustle sheep and turkeys nowadays and he gives a tithe to the poor."

"That's more on account of his stint in jail," said the first speaker of the errant ratcatcher. "Swore blind to the judge he thought they was rats!"

"Look at Josh Bell, he's the same. Stopped beating his missus and never touches strong liquor."

"And we all know how filled with the spirit he was afore he heard the Good News!" quipped the stockman. At this, the whole company roared with laughter and the sceptic condemned himself if he knew what the world was coming to when a man couldn't reach for the broomstale to keep his own house in order.

Just then, a pretty lass who had earlier caught William's attention fell into step beside him. She had twinkling eyes the colour of flax flowers and a blaze of copper-gold hair rippling from a filigree-trimmed cap which was one of three dozen she had made to hawk at market.

"I do know one thing," she offered shyly, "Mother's been able to make ends meet since she trusted the Lord. She don't need to lean on the Parish any more."

"And has she turned a Methodist?" William was intrigued.

"We all have," the girl told him. "Mother took us along to the Green, my three sisters and me - we didn't want to go, what with the stone-picking and thistle-cropping to do and the potatoes to plant for Mr Bowley - but we went and the preacher had us spellbound. Most particularly, I mind him sayin' that the Kingdom of Heaven was within every mortal person and that if we looked to that first, we'd not want for anything else again."

The young man's heart was strangely warmed by this artless testimony which his mother would eagerly have endorsed. Whilst he had the greatest respect for the Good Book and had tried to live by its precepts, was honest, hardworking and considerate of his fellows, he knew that he lacked the true spark of witness. His companion glowed with an inner assurance he did not possess.

She was called Abigail and William learned that she was named after a lady of quality for whom her mother had worked in her heyday. The Widow Reeve had no sons to ease her yoke. She had to take in heaps of mending and washing to stretch their threadbare budget. The Lord had cured her palsy and her fingers were nearly as nimble as they had been in youth.

Here, William realised, was a very practical faith, leavening the lives of ordinary people who chose not to venture inside a Parish Church to be scowled at by their betters. The bold few who did seek the Lord's Table would quite likely be discouraged by the vicar for whom swelling numbers meant less time at his own. He'd to make short work of his Sunday roast and port if he were to return promptly to conduct the afternoon service.

"I've heard tell of this Mr Wesley and the powerful good he has wrought up and down the land," William said.

"Come and see for yourself," Abigail invited. "There's a gospel meeting in Bowley's barn at sundown."

Sundown! That evening, there was a storm fit to sink Noah's Ark, though it did little to drown the fervour of the souls gathered in Farmer Bowley's leaking, ramshackle barn which reeked of musty timber. Nor could the darts of lightning and explosive thunder overwhelm their new hymns of praise. The simmering anticipation William had known during the day expanded into sheer elation. *"Let the fiery, cloudy pillar lead me all my journey through!"* he sang out in his confident baritone. He was at one in the fellowship of those whose hearts were sincere to the core. Abigail smiled up at him under the swinging lantern and there was an unearthly contentment in her eyes.

Suddenly, he felt immensely humble as it dawned upon him that hitherto his religion had been a relatively joyless affair. Of course, he had sought to make his corner of the world a better place, but a dedicated humanitarian in his shoes might have achieved even more. The Kingdom of Heaven could not be engineered; it could not be bought or earned. It was freely given to those who had the modesty to accept it through the Cross of Christ. Mr Bardsley, the itinerant preacher, spoke of faith as minute as a grain of mustard seed. When abandoned to the soil to await the season's quickening, it might flourish into a vigorous tree offering shelter to birds.

William returned home through the drenched darkness, his head spinning with brave new thoughts. "You look as though you've lost a farthing and found a sovereign," Abigail had teased.

"That's just it," William told her. "In a way, I have."

******

The summer waxed hot and the Wreake Valley wheat grew plump in the ear and lightened to gold. Larks boasted clandestine nests close to the marled earth. Fruit began to swell on the apple boughs and acorns to knot the clustered leaves of oak. The breeze blew where it would, unbeckoned, unseen, and William stirred with a sense of unfulfilled destiny.

There was no denying the bond between himself and Abigail. They reaped and sang and prayed together and it seemed as natural as breathing that their futures would intertwine. "I feel as though I've been born anew," he said to her.

"That is God's doing."

But William was a man with a man's hopes and dreams. "And yours," he ventured.

It all came to a head when the harvest was home and a ripe, round moon rode high in the sapphire twilight. The strains of a dozen dizzy fiddles leading the reapers and binders a merry dance at Farmer Bowley's supper carried far into the night amid shrieks of glee from the girls and bawdy hollering from the men. William took Abigail's hand and led her down the path to an old ash tree. Crop-dust and honeysuckle scented the air and the eternal earth felt firm beneath his feet. There, with the moon glittering through the feathery foliage, he clumsily declared his love and gave her a corn-dolly, symbol of fertility, he had crafted himself.

"I would bind you for ever like a sheaf of corn. Only say you'll be mine, Abby."

She pulled gently away from his impatient kiss. "What is it?" he said thickly. "What's wrong?"

"Will, there's something I have to tell you. I'm going away, over to Stapleford Hall…"

"But why?"

"Mother was in service there and they've found a place for me in the scullery."

"Your mother needs you here," he protested. "I need you!"

"What she needs is fewer to feed. We're all growing up, Will, working hard, eating more. We'll never have dowries to bring us fine husbands. We get by, but times are hard. There's scarcely a common left where you can graze a goat."

"But it's monstrous!"

She tried vainly to placate him. "I'll want for nothing, Will, and I'll be allowed home on Mothering Sunday and Saint Days."

Her sheer humility and her readiness to bow her head before her fate reminded him of nothing so much as a lamb going to slaughter. He could neither accept nor understand it. He drove his fist into his palm. "A scullery maid! Tis you who should be the lady!" he cried. "By heaven, Abby, I won't rest day or night till I've delivered you from that! I'll toil and scrimp until we can afford a cottage of our own and I can bring you home as my bride!"

****

William was as good as his word. Abandoning his books, he redoubled his efforts to make the smallholding prosper. He bought a brace of geese, risked one or two cattle to graze his rich Stilton cheese pasture, and some extra sheep. He was an astute judge of the Leicestershire breed developed by Mr Bakewell of Dishley Grange near Loughborough. They were small-boned with plenty of meat and the finest wool on their backs to be found anywhere in Britain. A Rotherby cotter had acquired one of the new-fangled stocking-frames which was something of a novelty on this side of the county and, William calculated, would provide a market on the doorstep for his wares.

As the equinox came with mist and frost in tow, he was eager to take a turn at pleaching the hawthorns in the valley's byways, for which he earned the princely reward of fourpence a chain. It was necessary to keep the hedgerows at a height huntsmen could safely clear. The Quorn was a notable body and the rich and famous came down from the highways of Mayfair to discover its coverts and scout around for lodges of their own, bringing trade and the chance of domestic service to the village communities.

Intertwining the whippy boughs, Will thought much of Abby. He missed her sorely but had an abiding sense of her which was a comfort and a spur. Now there was a goal in sight, not just the grinding need to eke out a living from one season to the next. His parents noted the determined gleam in his eye and exchanged wistful smiles, recalling their own salad days.

But if he neglected his books and his studies, William always spared time for worship. Every Sunday and many a weeknight, too, he would gather with those in the barn at Frisby-on-the-Wreake who were daily adding to their company. It was a godless place, an unlikely neighbourhood for the spiritual renascence taking hold in its midst. For performing unlawful rites of wedlock, the vicar had been sentenced to fourteen years transportation but was so feeble and frail that no magistrate bothered to see it enforced and he was allowed to slip into well-timed retirement. The church was in turmoil and the village ill-prepared for the new Dissenting creed which was taking it by storm. Its followers were taunted by hoodlums, sometimes had their homes ransacked and risked life and limb to attend the meetings. It was perhaps a sign of divine blessing that peacemakers should present such a threat to those around them. William would take a quick diversion from the footpath at the back of the barn and try to sidle in unseen, but was gently chided by Ann Brown, a Scottish butcher's wife from Melton Mowbray. She and her husband would walk the distance three times a week to hear the gospel expounded.

"We must stand up and be counted, Will. There'd be no Church at all if those first disciples had remained locked in the Upper Room. Pray for the power of the Spirit that you'll not be afraid to bear witness to the Lord."

"I mind she said much the same to me," twinkled James Brown, "when discretion seemed the better part of valour. In our town, they think we've a touch of the fairlies and want us put away, but Annie won't give the devil an inch. Nay, Jimmy, says she, there's no back way to heaven!"

Mr Wesley, the good lady reminded them, had suffered all kinds of harassment in the course of his ministry. The clangour of church bells had not drowned out his preaching, nor bloodthirsty mobs prevailed against him. In one Somerset village, a raging bull had been let loose and in Leicester a street crier had been posted to shout fresh salmon to the throng pressed into the Castle Yard. Rebels often attended such gatherings with pockets stuffed with rotten eggs 'less sweet than balsam', but nothing deterred the nimble little orator and no one could gainsay him. Whenever his faith was severely tested, he turned the situation to advantage so that his most vehement persecutors became his staunchest defenders. One such was John Massey, a notorious pugilist from the coalpits of north-west Leicestershire. Once smitten by a conviction of God, he laid down his truncheon, bade his gang follow suit and became a widely respected local preacher, drawing vast crowds to rallies of his own. "As the Apostle Paul makes clear, Will: our strength is made perfect in weakness when we trust in the Cross."

"Believers do have a way of turning the world upside down," said the lad with a wry grin.

"Nay, they set it steadfastly on its feet!"

In the fullness of time, William was invited to a service at the beautiful St. Mary's, Melton Mowbray, whose proportions and intricate masonry resembled a small cathedral.

"The parish church! I thought nothing would sway you from the Methodist persuasion!"

"Nor will it," Ann Brown stoutly declared, "but a most wonderful thing has come to pass. A new clergyman has been appointed to the living in Melton and what do you think, Will? - he knows John Wesley and has asked him to preach from the pulpit! There now!"

"They're as chieflike as mice in a cheese vat!" confirmed her spouse.

"What's more, he's a likely fellow concerned with the everyday needs of his parishioners and not afeared to speak his mind."

It turned out that the Revd Dr Ford was to make a strong impact on the grazier from Rotherby. He combined a sprightly wit and body with a missionary sense of purpose. Mounted upon a dusky mare, he would sing his way through Handel's Messiah during the journey from his rectory to Leicester and was full of admiration for the composer's forethought in having created a work of due length for such an excursion. Were he to travel blindfold, he claimed, he would know when he approached the town. The Hallelujah chorus always heralded his entry at Belgrave Gate!

Excitedly, Will wrote to Abby to tell her the news and promised that if she could get permission for Sabbath leave, he would take her to hear the Great Man at Dr Ford's church. Lately, when he had been able to see her, riding over to Stapleford to sit for an hour in the kitchen or walk in the parterre herb garden, he was perturbed to find her pale and thin with shadowy rings beneath her eyes. She rarely complained, but the sparkle of her personality had died and he prayed all the way home that God would help him expedite her deliverance. It was all of two years since she had gone into service - she had risen to the rank of second cook - but, as far as he could see, it might be another three before he had amassed enough savings for a small farm. The important thing in these unsettled days was ownership.

However, to the deep disappointment of the evangelicals, John Wesley replied that he was unable to wait upon his friend at Melton, having a diary packed with engagements for several weeks ahead. Instead, he proposed to send his trusted assistant, Revd Robert Carr Brackenbury of Raithby Hall in Lincolnshire, a landowner and magistrate whose abundance of this world's goods had not led him to share the dissolute life of many of his peers. Wesley had grown up at Epworth Rectory in the same county and the two families had been acquainted for generations.

And so, one radiant Sunday evening in September, William and the Browns found themselves drinking tea in Dr Ford's newly cream-washed and dragged drawing room in the company of his exalted guest. In the pulpit, he had delivered himself of an impassioned sermon on the value of laying a firm foundation, of building one's house on rock, taking for his text: *Christ, our Cornerstone.* The church was more than stone and oak and bright-hued glass, jewelled crucifix and silver chalice; it was the soul of its people. Only when faith prevailed, could the fabric of earthly life be maintained. King Solomon, seeking wisdom, had raised a temple to the glory of God where his father, King David, who had sinned, though he repented, had been unable to realise this dream.

Strangely, these images of construction made William's pulse race. He was in a fever to talk to this ambassador of Mr Wesley's.

"And how long is it, young man, since you were converted to Methodism?" Mr Brackenbury enquired.

"Why, it is more than two years, sir," William answered. "We meet in a barn a couple of leagues from here. We have repaired its beams and made it a respectable, if humble, place to sing hymns."

"Ah, there are many such scattered throughout the land. And some worthy converts have no roof but a spreading beech. It is not at all what our founding father envisaged. But then, his life has had another Architect."

"I don't quite follow, sir," William confessed.

The cleric's tawny-flecked gaze was warm and penetrating. "Mr Wesley's first love is the Anglican Communion. It was never his intention to break away. He wanted to set it by the ears, breathe life into a body paralysed by treating with pride. Alas, its doors are closed against him and the world itself has become his parish. Even at Epworth, he has long been an outcast and once preached the Resurrection standing on his father's tomb. A telling irony! Now every town and hamlet must have a chapel and our ministers must seek a Dissenter's licence. After all, Mr Wesley is gaining in years."

"He is as fit as a fiddle," interjected Dr Ford, smartly gobbling a madeleine cake.

"Certainly. He is not immortal, however."

"We shall not seek to fund a new chapel in this town during my incumbency," the Doctor of Divinity informed him.

"I am glad, sir. The people of Melton Mowbray will enjoy the best of all possible worlds. Like the master, you are a true ecumenical."

William himself had not been unduly concerned with stones and mortar, holding that the Lord looked upon the heart. Though he was uplifted by the monumental grace of the shire's parish churches, there was in him a streak of youthful iconoclasm to which Nonconformist ideals appealed. Listening to the visitor, he became sharply aware that Methodism was sinking deep roots. Thousands of people from shore to shore had split away from the orthodox church. It was right that they and their ministers should be recognised and have properly consecrated places of worship. They ought not to have to meet in secret like the anarchists they were taken for.

In Leicester," William said, "the Millstone Lane Tabernacle was once a tumbledown barn."

"Our mutual friend has preached there on occasion," Dr Ford told Brackenbury, "but is inclined to feel his labour better spent elsewhere. In this part of the country, there is little extreme poverty, but a heavy preoccupation with the marketplace. Hearts are not easy to turn. Now in Bristol, where I come from, the poor colliers clamour for spiritual food. They'd not so much as an alphabet between them until Wesley built them a school and, later, a chapel."

"Yes, he is a man dedicated to the welfare of the whole person. The cure of souls might be his primary aim, but he has written widely on natural medicine and has set up a free clinic for the sick at the Foundery, as well as an almshouse for the poor."

The Browns, who had been keenly interested in what had passed, asked what was meant by 'the Foundery'.

"It was once the home of the Royal Arsenal, just outside the City of London," Brackenbury explained. "Long ago, it fell into ruin after an explosion. Wesley bought the shell of the building and converted it into a chapel big enough to hold a congregation of fifteen hundred or more. I suppose you might call it his headquarters. The problem is - albeit a blessed one - that the society there has burgeoned wonderfully. Already new premises are needed. What we are witnessing, my friends, are the birthpangs of a sect which appeals to rich and poor alike. Think of that! Think of the impact it must make on our national life!"

The florid light of an Indian summer sunset poured through the dark cypresses outside and William felt that this was the most stimulating and exciting moment of his life. He saw that Methodists could not go on being content to gather in barns. They must have their own identity, their own house of God, and one that was worthy of him.

He looked down at his hands, calloused from the plough, the sinews corded from wrestling with stubborn sheep at shearing time and from long hours of wielding his hedger's billhook.

"I only wish I were in a way to help," he sighed.

****

William prayed: "Lord Jesus, you have said 'Ask and it shall be given.' Whatever good thing we petition in your name, you engage to grant us. Help me, then, to raise a living monument to your glory for those who have no place of worship."

His mother had warned him to be careful what he requested in prayer. The Lord never turned a deaf ear and would surely answer in the fullness of time. It was a hard and fast promise straight out of the pages of the Good Book.

"Then it's bound to be all right, isn't it?" he argued.

"Maybe it is and maybe it isn't," was her cryptic reply. "Best to ask that his will be done rather than put yourself and the Lord to the test. Sometimes we can't bear to have what we want."

"I want to achieve something great for God. Surely no harm can come from that."

No, she thought, no harm can come from it, not in the long run. But she was anxious about her son's motives. He was in danger of losing his humility. His work was no longer a major source of satisfaction and he had grown quick to anger at the petty frustrations of the daily round. Perhaps she had indeed been unwise to foster his intellectual pursuits, making him long for things he could not have. "There's many a road to the Lord's purpose," she said. "Be sure you take the one that proves his yoke is easy and his burden light."

Abby, on the other hand, was delighted when Will regaled her with details of his meeting Mr Brackenbury, spinning as fine a description of the cut of his coat, the iced fancy cakes and cowcumber sandwiches as of the substance of the conversation. "To think," she said dreamily, "that he and the Vicar are both hand in glove with Mr Wesley."

"If only I were rich, Abby, we could be married at once and have done with this drudgery. I could build a school and a dispensary for the sick. A church."

His eyes were flinty with pent-up frustration. It was only to be expected after so much unrelenting toil, Abby thought. She put down her basket of bay, lemon thyme and rue, inhaling the faintly damp fragrances of early autumn, and linked her arm through his. "We're simple folk, Will. Those grand ideas are not for the likes of us. But one day, we'll have a roof of our own. We'll have little ones and we'll bring them up to love and serve the Lord. We'll see that they're educated so that they can have the chances we never did. They'll be the doctors, the lawyers, the builders."

This vision of harmony and predestiny was suddenly appalling to William. He did not want his powers subsumed in the next generation. He wanted to accomplish great things himself. He thought: I am trapped. And the notion astonished and terrified him.

He broke away from Abby, then clasped her shoulders firmly. "I will do it," he vowed. And he could not tell whether it was futility or pity which moistened the fragile blue eyes. Untethered clouds hid the sun: she glanced at the shadowless sundial and then towards the blue-faced stable clock, shivering. "Tis fearful cold of a sudden," she said. "I must go in now. Time to prepare the master's supper."

They crossed the yard where he had left the dappled grey he'd borrowed from Sawyer, his neighbour. He kissed her on the forehead. "Goodbye, Will," she whispered. "Mind how you ride." His lordship of Harborough had set gintraps all over the estate to snare poachers and thieves in the night.

A HOUSE NOT MADE WITH HANDS

The skies opened. Rain thrashed and lashed the road ahead.

****

It was certainly a black Sunday. On the way home, Sawyer's mare threw a shoe and sprained her fetlock so that he had to lead her by the reins at a snail's pace. He arrived at Rotherby drenched and squelching to learn he had lost the wheat meadow that had gone unharvested. Next morning, it lay dank and beaten, fit for nothing. Moreover, he discovered the church tower at Melton had been struck by lightning and some severe damage done. During their devotions, the congregation had fled to safety with many dark utterances about the new Dissenters among them who had brought down the wrath of God.

William's mother coddled him with mustard footbaths and balsam possets when a fierce ague set in. "Never mind," declared she, stoical to the last, "it might have been *your* hind leg that gave way and we're fresh out of vinegar and brown paper!"

It was several days before the fever abated and he began stumbling about the farm, clattering pails and rolling churns, insisting that he must be about his tasks. He felt obscurely guilty about the wasted wheat, though it was sheer volume of work rather than indolence which had caused the delay. Increasingly, George Cooper's rheumatism made manual labour an ordeal for him and it became necessary for Will to take on a village lad named John Breedon who was as keen to learn his letters as he was to stack straw. George was often away visiting Hannah's cousin, Tom Kendal, in Syston, who was laid low with a liver disease. When she felt she could be spared, Hannah went with him, but that was not often since all able hands were needed at home.

The pair of them suffered many anxieties about Tom. Will's father and Sam Pickard, a fellow farmer from Syston, had even gone to the lengths of trundling poor Tom in a handcart down the footpath at the bottom of The Goose Neck which led across the fields to a spring known as St. John's Well. This, many believed, had curative properties, though the local apothecary said they'd have done better with more regular doses of his horehound syrup.

Tom fought valiantly, but it did not seem likely that he would recover. As the flame of life slowly dimmed within him, there were mutterings of wills, attorneys, the signing of documents.

All this washed over Will as he went about his duties. The ague had left him in a kind of limbo, as if the true atmosphere of his life had forsaken him. At the height of his delirium, he had been plagued by vivid dreams which revisited him as he swept the yard and mended the stile. With stark clarity, he had seen a fine temple, the work of his own hands, rising up to the heavens. He had wanted the whole world to catch its breath in admiration of its intricate beauty. But when the architect came to assess it, he condemned the foundations. The superstructure was unsafe and likely to collapse. "But I have done as you instructed!" Will protested in dismay. "I have built on rock!"

"Have you?" came the reply. "Then why does the very ground fracture beneath you?"

And looking down, he saw to his horror that the earth was not solid at all, but only hard-baked from drought. A chasm was opening under his feet. "The conception may be mine," said the architect, "but the design is yours. You have followed your own plan."

Emerging from the mists of sickness, he seemed to have lost his way. A vague sense of foreboding gnawed at him. Clumsily, he knocked over an earthenware flagon. It shattered into a dozen shards on the stone-flagged floor. There was little point in attempting to piece it together.

In the parlour, bent over his accounts whilst his mother sewed, he tried to reconcile the debits and credits. The startling sound of rent cloth made him look up and see her tearing a strip from a thinning shirt. "What's that you're doing?"

"I'm making a patch to mend the best shirt you tore on a briar."

"But you've that crisp square of lawn you bought at the market."

Mrs Cooper chuckled away to herself. "Son, tot up your figures and leave the making-do to me. If you had time to read scripture these days, you'd know well enough that the quickest way to rag worn cloth is to patch it with new."

"I don't see why."

"Because it's unshrunk, you great ninny! There's not much in this vale of tears that doesn't need bringing down to size before you can get the true measure of it.

"He did not care to consider this. He went off to see what could be salvaged of the despoiled crop. The sky was like tarnished metal. The air, still and echoing, threatened another storm. Honing his scythe, in preference to the slower sickle, he began to cut wider and wider swathes of stubble, scarcely stopping for breath or to mop the blinding sweat from his brow. In a ditch nearby, a fat ewe was bleating. The foolish creature had probably got itself stuck.

Suddenly, a hollow pain lanced through his chest. He reeled momentarily, leaning on his tool. His breathing came shallow and fast. A profound blackness seemed to engulf the whole universe, as though creation itself were severed from its Maker.

The moment passed. Will raised his water flask to his lips, then allowed its cool cleanness to sluice his face. A voice was calling from the pound. "Oh Will...! Oh son...!" He turned sharply at the tones of panic and distress.

"Mother, whatever is it?"

She was running towards him, skirts flying, bosom heaving, all her usual stolid command of the situation gone. "Tis Abby," she blurted out. "She fell sick of a fever like yours last week. Will, the Lord's taken her!"

****

He had half-expected her to say that his father had broken a limb or that Tom Kendal had gone to his forefathers. But Abby...!

He stood, as though turned to stone, in the middle of his ruined harvest. Then a shuddering cry tore through him. He sank to his knees, sobbing bitterly, laughing hysterically at the cruel irony of it. "What's it all been for? Dear God...why! Have I not been your faithful soldier and servant?"

****

A harsh winter followed. Icicles long as swords hung from the church tower and gave forked tongues to the grimacing gargoyles. The hawthorns stiffened and root crops tasted of frost. 'Scrapey' was rife among sheep. By now almost all the common land was enclosed. It angered Will that the poor had been put very much in their place.

Hannah, as always, was disposed to look on the bright side for, if they suffered some reverses, they were not actually in want. A touch of frost would mean a healthier growing season. "Besides," she added, "it makes for a very flavoursome parsnip!"

"If it doesn't put paid to them altogether," retorted Will gloomily.

She observed him sadly, understanding that he must give vent to his grief. "'Tis nature's way of renewing life," she said gently. "Pray that the Lord will sustain you."

"You need the patience of Job to be a Christian. Mother, I can't pray. I'm not sure I believe any more."

"Then go to your plough and let others do the praying."

"Yes," he sighed, "if we're to eat bread, I must." At the door he turned, twisting his crumpled hat in his hands. "Mother, I... I... loved her," he stammered brokenly. "It was she who drove me on. I wanted to rescue her, not leave her to die in that draughty pile."

"'Twas not in your power, son. Maybe those who look to God can never take glory for themselves, but they're spared the burden of guilt. Think what a comfort that is!"

"But I didn't do enough..."

"Perhaps you tried too hard. You trusted overmuch in your own strength."

"These times are devilish tough. It just seemed daft not to secure the future. The price of corn is enough to drive a man to the gin-palace!"

He put on his hat and strode out into the bleak December wind. Hannah watched him go. "Ah son," she whispered, "what you have to decide is whether you wish to possess or be possessed."

Will forced the plough through the unyielding earth so that he would not be behind at sowing time. He must do as his father had bidden and not look back. His hands were chapped and his breast ached but somehow it absorbed the bitterness and frustration. He supposed that if God did not hold him guilty, then neither could be reproach God.

As if the frozen ground were not trial enough, this particular field was riddled with stones. He had doled out twopence a bushel to the village ragamuffins for removing the worst of them.

And the crushing irony overwhelmed him.

"I have sought to raise wheat on stony ground and have reared my future on sand," he said to himself. "My life has been built on false premises."

****

Of course, it followed as the day the night and spring the winter, that the passage of time brought a soothing of grief and fresh expectation to Will. Swallows returned and the lilacs smelled sweet. His work became his salvation and he was content to replenish the earth and subdue it.

What had died, what had gone to the grave, was his Adam self. His mortal pain. His own conceit. Abby had gained a sublimer deliverance than he had prayed for. Perhaps he needed her eternal spirit to be his guide more than her presence in the flesh. He lit a candle for her at St. Mary's and watched the bruised, golden flame quiver and burn throughout the service.

That year, at the Millstone Lane Tabernacle in Leicester, he was privileged to hear Mr Wesley himself preach a fiery sermon on 'the house not made with hands'.

It was an uplifting occasion and marked the reconstruction William Cooper's life.

****

Troubles seldom come singly and the previous winter had been no exception. Will's distant cousin, Thomas Fletcher Kendal, had given up the battle with infirmity and was resting in peace at last. Now his attorney was laboriously engaged in proving the will made five years earlier. This was a sore trial to George Cooper, who, along with Samuel Pickard, a farmer colleague of the deceased, was named executor.

"At least Tom's females are well provided for," Hannah mused. "Aunt Mary and Cousin Elizabeth should be very comfortable."

"They're not exactly poor as Job's turkey, those two" said her husband, knocking out his ancient pipe on the andiron. "Tom's father was worth a tidy penny and his brother had his wits about him."

"To him that hath shall be given…!"

"Tis just as well, for we're unlikely to get things settled this side of next year."

Tom Kendal's principal asset was a small estate known as Whattoffe's House located in Town Street, Syston. This comprised of a sizable dwelling with yard, garden, orchard and outhouses. Tom desired that the property should be sold and the proceeds divided equally between his mother and sister. He had been unable to farm during his chronic illness and doctors' fees and druggists' bills had been a constant drain upon his purse so that, in order to gain maximum revenue, he'd had the house converted into three tenements. George feared that in its present state, the house would be a less attractive proposition to a buyer. Months of pettifogging probate would also mean a hefty slice of the cake for the lawyers.

By October, Whattoffe's House was on the market with three sitting tenants. It was advertised by poster on the village green, The White Swan, a coaching inn on the Leicester Road, and in the county's broadsheet, the Leicester and Nottingham Journal. There was a modest flurry of interest which soon fizzled out with no firm offer. Since the building was in good repair and the land well-tended, George could only surmise he'd been right.

"In Sam Pickard's opinion, twould make a very sound investment." He was wedging a stout log into the fire when Will burst into the kitchen, eager for supper.

He kissed his mother. "What's that, then?" he asked, catching the tail of the conversation.

"Cursed place of Tom's off Brook Street. We'll be lucky to bag a sale in a month of Sundays."

"You need some fine fellow to come along who's keen to make hay with property."

George eyed the lad shrewdly for a moment or two. "Tis a pity no one in the family's in a way to bid for it. Tis a particular pity, that."

"Why so? Better to swell Great Aunt Mary's coffers with foreign money."

Almost dissembling, George said brusquely: "No sense of the past, no pride in your heritage, you youngsters. Your great grandfather bought that house from William Whattoffe not long after Queen Anne was crowned. And a rundown heap it was, too! Three generations of Fletchers have made it what you see today."

"I've never given it a thought, I own."

"Tough as Methuselah he was. Outstayed his welcome, some said."

"Yes, I dimly recall the old stager. He was as deaf as a scarecrow."

"Now *he* was an ardent Protestant," Hannah interrupted. "He called your grandfather and great aunt after King William and Queen Mary who came over from Holland to knock the Old Pretender off his perch."

"Lived to bury your grandfather," George added. "That's how Whattoffe's estate came to pass to Tom Kendal, your mother being on the distaff side."

Out in the fields, sowing the winter grain, Will cast his mind on those who had gone before. A door had opened on a new perspective of the past and future. His life was peopled with ghosts. He thought of his ancestors who had lived and died in the faith and of the brevity of the human span in the perpetual cycle of the seasons. He was a mere strand in the tapestry that would strengthen the weave or leave it threadbare for following generations to try to make good. Suddenly, it mattered intensely to him that Whattoffe's House should not be sold to a stranger.

"Father," he said resolutely that night, "I've a notion to purchase Tom's house, then it shan't be lost to this family."

The withered old farmer looked pleased but cautious. "Have you counted the cost, Will?"

"What savings I have must be put to usury, not buried under the floorboards. You ask a hundred and ten sovereigns. I have a hundred and three. Will you accept that?"

George clapped a hand on the lad's shoulder. "Son, I will! And I'll tell you something for nothing: you'll never have cause to repent of this day's deed."

And so it was, in the Year of Grace, seventeen hundred and seventy-seven, that William Cooper became the new owner of Whattoffe's House.

"Will's a man of property now," his mother fairly boasted. "He discovered the treasure and bought the whole field!"

****

For the next ten years, William continued to till the land and abide with his parents. Autumn by autumn, as his endeavours came to fruition, he was able to record a neat profit. He acquired a dozen head of Dishley Longhorn cattle and a share in a winnowing-fan to speed up the process of separating grain from chaff.

There were as many new devices to improve methods of farming as there were machines to take over the old cottage industries. Artisans began to make tracks for the towns and cities. There was work to be had in the dour factories being spawned on wasteland and watermeadow. After a hard-won war, the American Colonies had claimed independence and Mr Pitt, addressing the thorny problem of debt, launched measures which bit deep into the economy and made only a topsy-turvy sort of sense. For instance, a tax on servants, levied on the rich, meant unemployment for many a poor retainer. The window tax prompted thousands of freeholders to swallow up the smaller premises to which their inferiors aspired, or else set about bricking out the light of day.

Throughout England, the first fledgling chapels began to alter the skyline. In Leicester, The Tabernacle which had done such sterling duty since its days as a shed, was finally pulled down and a smart new Preaching House erected. The original panel of trustees included one, William Cooper of Rotherby, a gentleman becoming widely renowned in Methodist circles for the strength and style of his testimony. He had not neglected his friends at Frisby-on-the-Wreake and, with the support of Jamie and Ann Brown, he set up a society in Great Dalby after inviting the itinerant preachers Benjamin Squire and Walter Sellon to testify there.

Alongside William Cooper, as a trustee of the Millstone Lane Preaching House, was John Coltman, the master hosier whose long habit it had been to catch up with John Wesley during his travels through the county. Since his youth, he had been a convinced Nonconformist and the passing years had done nothing to diminish his fervour.

At that time, the hosiery trade, which was the chief one in Leicester, was hampered by a fierce tide of Radical idealism. Wherever you turned, there was antagonism towards progress. Fear of change and wage losses warred with the desire for a brighter future and improved working conditions. It was true that the same discontent was echoed in many other towns, but the denizens of Leicester had an unhappy knack of standing in their own light. They had it in their gift to be at the leading edge, blessed as they were with nimble fingers, quick wits and expertise. What they did not possess was vision.

In 1787, the low rumble of grievance which had gone on since the early seventies, caused by poor harvests and a dramatic falling-off of trade with America, erupted into fullscale revolt. The butt of their anger was a fast new worsted spinning machine developed by Joseph Brookhouse, a business colleague of Coltman's. The two men and a third party, Joseph Whetstone, Nonconformists all, had put their heads together to exploit the new invention which they believed could make the town the hosiery mecca of the world.

"They might as well chop off their own hands, this purblind mob!" stormed Brookhouse, pacing his oak-panelled office behind a firmly locked and bolted door. "Can they not see that our objective is to create wealth and secure employment for this benighted town?"

Outside, the winter night was crisp and the sky thickly broadcast with a frosty glittering of stars. A spirit of revenge had taken hold among the seething crowd in the street below and it would not be long before they were baying for blood.

"Would that Wesley were here. He would know how to quieten them," shuddered Coltman.

"Wesley does not strive with our problem," replied the other testily. "He cries his message and departs. Our livelihood, and theirs, if they could but grasp it, is at stake. They cling to their fear and ignorance like a talisman."

"Ay, there'll be little bread tomorrow, let alone dripping, if we cannot persuade them. Dear Lord, I wish that lad would make haste."

They had sent a porterhouse boy scurrying off with a note for the Mayor and the rabblerousers had begun laying siege to the door. A swelling bellow, like an injured and demented lion unleashed, filled the night, followed by a concerted thundering of labourers' boots and clogs. "Come out! Come out, Brookhouse!" they chanted. "Let's see what you're made of!"

"Ye'll not shift us in a hurry!" bawled a rough-throated watchman, wielding a torch in menacing fashion. "We've got Whetstone's pad surrounded and if he don't do as he's bid, we'll turn the place over and dispose of him as neat as may be."

Goaded now, Brookhouse rashly wrenched up the window and thrust out his head. "Hold your peace, Turnbull, you insolent brute! The Mayor and his henchmen are coming and will have you flung behind bars for insurrection."

Turnbull guffawed mockingly. "Hark at him, lads! Do ye hear? If my aim was as smart as his blether, I'd set the whole building ablaze and have done. Where is he, then, the Mayor? I don't hear His Worship's eager footfall on the path. He wants no truck with a bloody Liberal like you, Brookhouse. You and your ilk would jackboot him out of office as soon as look at him. He's a Tory diehard and he's on our side!"

"For God's sake, Joe, pull down the window and come away." pressed Coltman. "The loathsome fellow has a point, has he not? Where is the Mayor? He's certainly in no hurry to impose order on these streets."

His companion tugged at his necklinen and tossed it aside, panting angrily. "Politics makes strange bedfellows, to be sure." Leaning back against the wall, out of sight, he glanced at the longcase clock in the corner. "It is an unconscionable length of time - near five and forty minutes - since we despatched the serving-lad to the Mayor's chambers."

"The young scapegrace has probably run off with his shilling. Do you suppose he reached his destination?"

"It scarcely matters now. This uproar will be heard far and wide and those in authority will soon learn the cause of it."

Just then, a pebble struck one of the small leaded panes, dead centre, and fractured it into a neat spider's web. The clamour abated into a handful of catcalls. "What the Hanover…?" Around the corner, the civic carriage, emblazoned with the town's crest, hove into view and rattled to a halt in Shambles Lane fifty yards or so from the master hosier's premises. A postilion jumped down and rushed to open the door so that His Worship in ceremonial finery could alight armed with his warning scroll. In a shaft of bronze light, the two comrades saw that he appeared more inconvenienced than wrathful. He was a corpulent, whey-faced figure, fond of his liquor and the trappings of his role. He had been summoned from a banquet and was keener to get back to his charlottes and syllabubs than to quell a riot. "Come, my lads, give over… You've done enough, quite enough. Come, give over, there's good lads and go away!"

They had sent a mouse to bruise the head of a lion. The mob was in no mood for these inept babblings. It was as wild-eyed as a primitive beast.

A welter of protest broke out afresh. A grisly hulk of a man picked up one of the granite setts laid out for new paving and hurled it with olympian force toward the dignitary where it struck directly between his shoulder blades. The victim swayed, staggered and slumped to the ground while the crowd pressed in upon him with a heady mixture of panic and elation.

"Dear Heaven!" exclaimed Brookhouse, "I reckon they've done for him! Come on, Jack, now's our chance!"

"Tis madness, stark madness," quaked the other. Nevertheless, caution abandoned, they flew down the staircase, fumbled frantically with the doorlatch, and gained the pavement just as a pallet was being brought out of a nearby house to cart the casualty off to the infirmary. His writhing groans told them all was not lost. But the rebels had got their scapegoat and were momentarily stunned, until a sense of failure overtaking them, their blood rose again and they seized the opportunity to storm the hosier's house, battering window-frames, vaulting the sills, swarming through the open door and up the stairs, and with truncheons, bargepoles, gridirons, anything to hand, set about wreaking a frenzy of destruction, the blood-smeared Riot Act trampled to a pulp beneath their feet.

By the time it was borne in upon them that Coltman and Brookhouse had fled, the two men were absorbed in the mêlée outside and made good their escape across the Castle Yard toward the dimly illumined windows of St. Mary de Castro where some kind of Advent Mass was taking place. Tiptoeing into the incense-laden gloom, they sought sanctuary, quiet as mice, behind a pillar in the shadowy recesses of the ancient church, trying to still their rasping breath and thanking God for their fleetness of foot.

The service over, they dared to emerge. There were still echoes of disturbance around the streets, but it was quieter and an air of futility lay over the town, thick as fog. Every alehouse was packed to bursting, spilling its patrons, in various stages of inebriation, on to the pavement. News of the riot was on everyone's lips and the hosiers soon learned that some arrests had been made and that their confederate, Whetstone, had also had his house ransacked but had eluded the mob, like a true apostle, in a basket from an upper window. It was now common currency that he had applied to the Town Hall for protection in advance of the attack and had received none.

"This is an evil night's work," Brookhouse lamented with barely controlled tears when the devastation of Shambles Lane made its impact. "It is plain there is no future here for me and my machine."

"What will you do?"

"I am resolved to take it elsewhere - into a neighbouring county, I fancy - and let others reap their good fortune with it."

"But the whole industry will dwindle and die without it."

"Try telling them that!" cried Brookhouse, waving an arm at the ghost of the enraged throng. "Try telling the Mayor and Corporation. They were by no means keen to defend us, honest taxpayers or no."

"Perhaps Turnbull was right. They do fear our political muscle. But if we are a force to be reckoned with, we are gaining ground. You must stay and do battle, Joe."

"Indeed, I cannot. You forget that a full century has passed since the days when Dissenters were first allowed to hold municipal office, thanks to the Huntingdon family who have done so much to pave Wesley's way. A hundred years! And still it is an Anglican Tory stronghold. Ay, and likely to remain so until it becomes a democratically elected body. It is as clear as crystal that they dare not go against the will of the rabble if they are to keep a purchase on their power."

Coltman thought this a defeatist speech, but did not say so. "This town," he said sadly, "could be one of the jewels of England. Its pastures are the richest, its cheeses world-renowned, its mutton the envy of Smithfield. It has a thriving brick industry, its fine black Shire horses are the pride of the country's coaching routes, hosiery has rescued the pauper from beggary…"

"Yet is has no vision, no faith." Brookhouse restored a chair to its upright position amid the debris and sank into it, clutching his head in his hands. "The time has come for workers to adapt their skills. The days of the cottage knitting-frame are numbered. The future lies in large manufactories. If the knitters were not so stubborn, they would see it is the only way to ensure food on the table, shoes on the feet of their children, decent working conditions and, perhaps, reduced hours of labour. They demand a minimum wage of knitmasters like you and me, but how are we to guarantee that without changing our methods? The whole operation is patchy and unprofessional."

"First they must be persuaded that the machine is their friend. Since you are concerned about the welfare of the townspeople, have you not a Christian obligation to stay and do so?"

"Oh no, Jack, that is not my reading of the case at all. There is nothing Christian about clinging to the past. It is a way of faith. As New Testament disciples we are called upon to shake the dust off our feet, not cry in the wilderness. Leicester's motto is well chosen. *Semper Eadem.*

****

The death in hospital of the Worshipful Mayor cast an even darker shadow on this chapter of events. The upshot was that Joseph Brookhouse packed his belongings and took his brainchild off to Warwickshire where it was welcomed. This was to prove a major stumbling block to progress and it would be many years before the trade regained its feet. As a piece of editorial in the Leicester Journal stated: *'Two of these machines are said to have been destroyed. Violence and intemperate riot may prevent its operation, but also drive away the whole manufacture.'*

"We had hoped that Brookhouse would suffer a change of heart," Coltman told William Cooper at a trustees' meeting, "but it was not to be expected with so unhappy an outcome."

"These are unstable times," said William gravely, "as our Gallic neighbours know to their cost."

It was indeed a time of ferment. The King himself realised how much he owed the indefatigable Mr Wesley when widespread rioting could so easily have escalated into the anarchy and bloodshed going on across The Channel. The aging preacher had continued his awesome tours of the British Isles, never flinching from a punishing routine which required him to rise at four in the morning. In London, his latest chapel of grand and classical proportions in the City Road, had a growing membership which included the well-educated and high-ranking. His Majesty had donated masts from the naval dockyard at Deptford to be used as pillars for the gallery. Methodism was at last becoming respectable.

So, while the newly metalled roads accelerated the pace of travel and smart mail coaches hogged the crown of the highway, a different brand of Christian witness was staking its claim in the nation's history.

As for William Cooper, the pattern of his existence looked set to continue for ever. That was until the day he discovered his father slumped against an overturned milk pail.

3

The Sown Seed

1790

"And to think I never knew that father was a man of means," marvelled Will, peering through a sullen November drizzle from the parlour window.

Apparently George Cooper had inherited a house and five closes in Brook Street, Syston, some years ago, and had seen fit to keep the fact dark. His son was now to receive an unexpected legacy.

"We'd made our bed here," said Hannah. "We'd no cause to go changing our ways so late in the day. Your poor father was always a 'doer'. He made no pretence of being a gentleman."

Though her eyes glistened as brightly as ever, she looked withered and drawn, not long for this life herself.

It was a week since the yeomanly grazier had been laid to rest in Syston churchyard in the shelter of a spreading beech tree not far from the vestry door. He and Hannah had been married at St. Peter's and cherished the wish to be buried there. Now the last will and testament had been read, the baked meats consumed, the farewell respects offered by family and friends. Widow and son were left to pick up the thread of their lives as best they might.

"It's odd how matters have turned out," Will said. "He must have realised that the property adjoins Whattoffe's House."

"Ay, it gladdened his heart when you made up your mind to that. But he wanted you to act of your own accord."

"The question remains: what now?"

"You always did have half a fancy to be a gentleman."

"My stake in the world has redoubled overnight. We've no longer any need to delve and spin."

"Your Da was keen you should learn the lore of the land. Many's the time he upbraided me for encouraging you to fill your head with clever nonsense, but I doubt not there's a place for that too in the Lord's plan."

Will turned away from the window and, sitting beside her on the arm of the sofa, possessed himself of her bony hand. "It's what the future's about, Ma," he said earnestly. "Education for all. It's everyone's birthright. Then the upper classes shan't have the upper hand."

"The world's changing so fast, I scarcely know what to make of it." A bewildered sigh escaped the old lady. "It won't be the same here without… him."

"Then what say you we upsticks and make our home in Brook Street? You were born and bred in Syston."

"We'd be near your Da's resting-place," his mother said, brightening a little.

"The premises are much bigger than we're accustomed to, but just think what it could mean. We could entertain a host of travelling preachers, extend the Methodist church, create a place of worship under our own roof."

Hannah drew her shawl more closely around her. "I don't know… Tis a heathen place, though I say it as shouldn't. God-fearing folk are thin on the ground in Syston."

"Then isn't that where we ought to be. Is it not what God expects of us. That house stands empty and idle since Mr Harcourt left."

"Your Da knew his day was nearly done."

"The want of a tenant is surely a sign."

Swayed by her son's eloquence, old Mrs Cooper agreed to the move, convinced that no good could come of resisting. She had already exceeded her allotted span and had lived in Rotherby for forty-four years. Where she might have clung on to the familiar like a life-raft, she was prepared to let go.

Under no circumstances would William have left her and she did not want to stand in his way. Had she not foreseen that a time would arise when the seed planted long ago would come into season?

A faint amusement gleamed through her sadness. "He never lets up, Him Upstairs. Always wants us to go the second mile and give the cloak off our backs."

"Then do as you've always done, dearest Ma. Consider the lilies!"

****

By the Feast of the Epiphany, they were installed with their few goods and chattels in number 9, Brook Street, which had formerly been occupied by a surgeon.

Early in March, they received the dispiriting news that their guide and mentor, John Wesley, had gone to his Maker, united after a space of three years with his brother, Charles, who had written a prodigious number of stirring hymns. Mr Robert Carr Brackenbury had been at his bedside.

"Best of all," Wesley had whispered, "is God is with us."

****

'I am sending you out like sheep among wolves.'

The text fixed itself in William's mind. What the Wesleys had left behind was the solid framework of a sect which was already organised into seventy-five circuits throughout England and Wales with a membership of some seventy thousand souls. What they had meant to do was to inspire a revival which would drive converts back to the Church of England. To their last breath, they were dedicated Anglicans whose very ardour had been construed as heresy. Their followers were harangued by the mob for promoting peace and persecuted by the Establishment for appealing to the mob. Seditious pamphlets like Mr Paine's *Rights of Man* had now been devoured by miners, cotters, weavers and rag-pickers. While revolutionaries learned from their French counterparts how to incite unrest, rioters were being called upon to defend their country against the French. Some were press-ganged into the Navy; many took the King's shilling to escape debt, hunger and responsibility for their families.

"We must be as diligent as Wesley in keeping the ship on an even keel," William announced with an air of resolve, closing his broadsheet one morning. "Down the ages, Christians have been accused of causing wars: we must show that what's done in the name of faith seldom has aught to do with what's done in the name of religion. The common people have had a raw deal, but they must not run away with the notion they've been given leave to overturn the order of things."

"Twas they who put Christ to death," reflected Hannah.

"Twas lack of commitment put Christ to death! Hosannas on Palm Sunday: crucifixion on Good Friday!"

In his efforts to see the gospel proclaimed in the neighbourhood, William needed all the crusading zeal he could muster. At every corner he met with antagonism and often downright hostility. Next door, in what was known as The Olde House, there lived a young surgeon, Matthew Dalley. He had lately arrived from Somerby to fill the gap left by Mr Harcourt. This gentleman proved to be a trusted ally of the Methodist cause. He was built like an ox and was noted for his valour in the face of danger. Frequently he would act as a guard to visiting preachers and prevent disturbance among the crowd. On one particularly ugly occasion when a drunken framesmith from Sileby ran wild with a meat cleaver, it was Matthew who restrained him while the converted called upon the Lord to becalm the man's spirit and open his heart. Their intercession worked better than a charm, for he and his family were to become buttresses of the faith.

Despite this, there was a small but expanding group of regular worshippers, about two dozen in all, who needed a sanctuary. Though William could offer hospitality to itinerant preachers and open his drawing-room for prayer and Bible study, he could not administer the Sacrament. This rite, along with weddings, baptisms and burials, must be performed by ordained clergy. Two villagers had latterly applied for Dissenters' Licences so that their homes might be used for public worship and had been refused.

The situation vexed him day and night. Years ago, when he had first experienced that intoxicating fellowship among Methodists, the lack of a church building had not mattered. Now it seemed an end devoutly to be wished. "Dear Lord," he prayed on his knees, "you know that your children need a house in which to honour you. Grant this good thing they ask in your name. Make the crooked path straight and the rough places plain."

"Will," sighed his mother, "I remember the time you'd a mind to raise a shrine to the glory of God all on your own."

"I was young and idealistic then. I needed to be brought down a peg."

"The aim was good but the motive wasn't the best. Not when you'd pledged yourself to Abigail, God rest her."

William looked discomfitted and Hannah saw that the old wound was still tender. "She has been overmuch in my thoughts of late. I… I wish our last meeting had been different."

"Rest assured, she knows your plight. She will be interceding for you."

"We need the prayers of the Church Militant and the Church Triumphant," he agreed hopefully. "We no longer have to live hand to mouth but that heroic dream is as far off as ever. For one thing, building costs are ever rising."

"When more people join us, we could raise a subscription."

"What we really need is the goodwill of one or two wealthy folk."

****

One hot Sunday around Lammastide in 1796, William took it into his head to walk to Melton Mowbray. He had a hankering to take Communion in Dr Ford's church and to hear one of his stimulating sermons. It was several years since the two had met and the eccentric Rector embraced William warmly and took him home to a duck dinner after the service. There the guest poured out his heart.

"I shall make it the highlight of my devotions," promised Dr Ford. "And I'll write to Brackenbury too. He will be interested to hear what you propose. He has been much impressed by what has been achieved at Millstone Lane in the town."

In lighter mood, William retraced his steps along the dusty turnpike, equipped with a flask of lemon cordial which the Rector's good lady had prepared for him. The sun was beating down and a mirage-like haze rippled off the ripe corn. After a while he decided to rest and refresh himself and entered a meadow to seek shade of a sycamore tree. Leaning against its bole, he swallowed some of his drink and contemplated the dip and rise of the fields which were, by now, entirely fenced in. Forgive us our trespasses, he thought wryly. He took a linen-bound pocket book of Scripture from the coat he had been carrying over his shoulder. Turning to the Sermon on the Mount, he read the Lord's Prayer and continued to follow the gospel of Matthew, the tax-gatherer. *'Again, the kingdom of heaven is like unto treasure hid in a field; the which when a man hath found, he hideth, and for joy thereof goeth and selleth all that he hath, and buyeth that field.'* There, William halted. The words had a tantalising ring, though he did not know why. Even as he absently closed the small volume, it fell open again at a well-worn passage from the first book of Chronicles. *'And David said to Solomon his son, Be strong and of good courage, and do it: fear not, nor be dismayed: for the Lord God, even my God, will be with thee; he will not fail thee, nor forsake thee, until thou hast finished all the work for the service of the house of the Lord.'*

With a pang of excitement, he got up to stride out again. The piece from Matthew brought sharply to his mind a remark his mother had made long ago when he had purchased Whattoffe's House. "I'm glad you saw that it was precious, Will. I'm glad you bought the whole field."

Whattoffe's House! Had be been blind? Since it had been converted into three separate dwellings, he had regarded the estate purely as a source of income. What he had overlooked was the derelict orchard behind his own garden! The trees badly wanted pruning and whitewashing, but each August they produced a crop of four or five bushels of sound Syston Whites, a succulent cross between a greengage and a goldendrop plum. Through a vanishing mist, he saw how that parcel of ground might be cleared to accommodate a little chapel and yield fruit of a different kind. If funds did not have to be found for the land, he would be able to contribute a fair sum towards the cost of the building. The venture would then be more likely to appeal to other benefactors.

At the end of the week, he took counsel with some of his firmest friends. There was Matthew Dalley, his neighbour, John Gregson, attorney's clerk and Will Rawson, hosier, both from Leicester, James Main, apprentice cordwainer from Rearsby, John Breedon, the dependable farmhand whom he had employed and educated during his latter years in Rotherby, and Robert Carr, another hosier who was also a notable Methodist preacher and an old associate of Wesley's.

Clustered around the Coopers' grainy elm dining-table, they asked for blessing upon their meeting and drew up a plan of campaign. The design and dimensions of the projected Preaching House were outlined and put out to tender so that they might quickly discover how far they fell short of their target.

Examining his finances, William found he could scrape together as much as four hundred pounds if certain economies were made. But when the quotations began to drop through his letterbox, it was obvious that nearly twice the sum was needed. However, nothing would daunt him now. Will Rawson, for one, had promised a donation.

"It is as though a cloud has lifted," he told his mother.

"The Lord always provides when he sees you mean business," she said, squinting down at her crochet hook. "There's nought betwixt and between about the Parable of the Talents!"

Sure enough, she was right. It was All Saints Day and their sixth winter in Syston when William brought a letter to the breakfast table and broke the wax seal. "It's from Brackenbury."

"I can tell as much from the frank," his parent said tersely, a trifle peeved at being kept in suspense when William's countenance was patently beaming.

"He wants to know what progress we have made in the matter of the church building. He engages to do what he can to help."

"Hallelujah!" cried Hannah. "Ay, but he's taken his time!"

****

It was in 1797, the year they built the bridge over the fast-flowing brook linking the Wreake and the Soar at Syston, that William Cooper's long cherished dream materialised.

Till then, pedestrians had made do with an oaken footbridge while carts and swaying coaches had gone splashing down into the ford, dragging precariously through its pebble bed as they charged towards the Toll Bar Gate further along Leicester Road. A steady increase in the pressure of traffic and the demand for faster travel had made a sturdy stone bridge essential. So important was this artery and so keen the desire not to inconvenience the public, that the whole structure was completed by nine men in nine days. They set to work with a will, shifting a mountain of twenty-five thousand bricks and a hundred and fifty tons of stone with such legendary despatch that their handiwork became known as the Nine Days Wonder.

If the bridge was to make plain the path of the body, the chapel was to ease the journey of the spirit.

Perhaps William Cooper's achievement was less of a miracle to the outward eye, but to those who understood the conflicts which had given birth to it, every bit as staggering.

By harvest time, work was in progress. The last batch of plums had been gathered. The trees were cut down and burned and gave off a smoke as sweet as incense to William. Next, the ground was dug out and the cornerstone and foundations blessed. Brick by brick, the walls rose under the blue-and-gilt October sky, the row of lanky poplars behind whispering approval. Soon the skeletal timbers were capped with slate and two arched windows fixed above the altar so that the light would stream down upon the communicants. Craftsmen were brought in to install the organ, the carved pulpit and finely turned galleries.

"That is where the Sunday School children will sit," William announced, showing his mother around. "We have not forgotten the youngsters."

"Will, it's grand! Tis all falling out as it should. I only wish your Da could see it. He'd be that proud."

"I don't doubt he can. And Abigail, too."

"Ay, they'll be conspiring up yonder, you can count on it!"

It was all he could do to restrain his mother, frail and bent as she was, from carrying a pail of water and a lemon up the ladder to wash the windows. She took good care, however, to see that all the brass fixtures and fittings were burnished as bright as could be and chivvied the wives who had come to polish the pews.

On Christmas Eve, all was finished. A milestone, a monument. A week later, before the Watch Night Service to usher in the new year, the congregation crowned their success and good fortune with a dedication by the Revd Robert Carr Brackenbury. The pillar candles shone with beatific radiance, the organ swelled with sacred music, the voices rose in glad thanksgiving:

> *See the Gospel Church secure*
> *And founded on a rock;*
> *All her promises are sure;*
> *Her bulwarks who can shock?*
> *Count her every precious shrine,*
> *Tell to after-ages, tell,*
> *Fortified by power divine,*
> *The Church can never fail.*

Old Mrs Cooper brushed a tear from her cheek and glimpsed the unaccustomed brilliance of her son's eyes.

"This is my memorial," he said, "my Bethel on the way to Canaan."

****

William was glad ever afterwards that his mother had lived to see him achieve his goal. At Michaelmas, 1799, she slipped on the stairs and fractured her thigh-bone which left her weak and in considerable pain. From her bed she watched flame-coloured leaves detach from the trees and knew with peaceful certainty that her time had come. "I'm going to your Da, Will," she whispered. "I've done with fretting that we've been apart for so long." One afternoon in late October, as the light was fading, she stole quietly away to join the ranks of the redeemed.

Though her life had been richly spent and her rest deserved, William was disconsolate throughout that dark and draughty winter. "I did not realise how much I owed her," he mourned. "She succoured me body and spirit."

In due course, he took Mary Wollett, a mature spinster and chapel-goer, into his home as housekeeper. She was keen to be of service and cared for him well, but was not endowed with his mother's sanguine temperament. News of lost battles and crimes perpetrated to keep the wolf from the door, which might incur the gibbet or transportation, formed the staple of her gossip. "There's no telling when this war will end," she grumbled as she flicked a malevolent goosefeather duster about the picture frames. "We'll all be poor as church mice till Kingdom come. It's no wonder the men are running off to give Boney a hiding with meat and free gin for the taking."

Britain's relations with France had served to reinforce the plight of the poor. The French had guillotined their King and Queen, declared a Republic and war on the British Empire. Napoleon, the Corsican Monster, was fighting his way tooth and nail across the upper hemisphere and in 1804 had the hubris to crown himself in Notre Dame with a gold laurel wreath like an archaic Greek hero. It was a tragedy that hard on the heels of earlier quarrels and famines came an even more ruinous enemy. Food was scarce, trade was slack, merchant ships lay idle or were requisitioned for the Fleet. Overseas markets were closed. Nor could the ruling party afford to sympathise: the slightest whisper of discontent was instantly stifled.

Thus the stability of the nation came to depend upon reformers and almsgivers, the prayers of believers, those of selfless principle and genuine compassion.

The Methodist Church was now a distinct entity with a second or third generation of itinerant ministers and a scattering of clergy drawn from the Anglican fold. Whether rightly or wrongly, John Wesley had committed a definite act of schism when, in attempting to make disciples of all nations, he had himself conferred Holy Orders on the Welsh pastor, Thomas Coke, who was bound for America. Furthermore, he had given him authority to perform the same rites on others.

"Wesley should not be blamed," said Matthew Dalley over supper with William the night they heard that Napoleon Bonaparte had been captured and imprisoned on Elba. "The Church has no fire in its belly. It answers neither the spiritual nor material needs of the lower classes. Nonconformists are doing the lion's share of the work."

"It is grievous that these things cannot be accomplished within the Anglican Communion. It is, after all, our heritage. How can it stand so aloof?"

The subject occupied William's mind day and night and was underlined by a particular experience in the village.

It was his custom to put by at least a tenth of his income for the work of God in and around the parish. He had helped to set up a number of Sick Clubs, but the problem with them was that subscribers could frequently not afford to keep up their dues.

Learning of the acute distress of the Cart family, he paid them a visit. A prolific household, they were crammed into a tiny cottage that had to accommodate a rented stocking frame. Last winter, Thomas Cart, the father, had met with a disastrous accident. Faint from exhaustion and the sloe gin consumed to stave off pangs of hunger, he had lost his balance and slumped into the machine which was being operated by William, one of his sons. The result was a ghastly wound to his forearm which his wife bathed in rainwater and dressed with strips of cloth from a ripped-up apron. "Lord 'ave mercy!" she shrieked, "What next? This will have to do, Tom. I daresn't go callin' the doctor in case he charges us."

Luckily, a major artery had been narrowly missed, but when the blood was eventually staunched, the injury festered, gangrene set in and he lapsed into a fever. Then Cathy fled in panic to hammer on Matthew Dalley's door. "Please, please, Dr Dalley, sir, come quick as you can! My poor hubby's done himself a terrible mischief and is mortal sick of a fever!" Fortunately, Matthew was a philanthropic soul and readily obliged. While Cathy wept copiously and sucked her knuckles, Tom was tied to the kitchen table and the putrid limb sawn off. Matthew gave her sixpence to buy bread and bones for broth and was gratified to see Tom recover with amazing speed. But he soon grew frustrated and morose at the misfortune which had unmanned him and it was rumoured he had lately taken to opium.

"How are you managing, Cathy?" asked William as the flustered matron surrendered her threshold to reveal a room pent with low black beams. He noticed how the grime of poverty had the same cankerous smell as well-handled coins.

"Oh, Mr Cooper, if we can stay out of the workhouse, that's all I ask. A bit of extra darning and washing and childminding sees us through now that Harry's out learning the wool combing."

Harry was Henry, the eldest of the brood, a solemn lad close on twenty. The rhythmic din from the next room was evidence that his brother was hard at work on the frame.

"What a blessing that William's an industrious fellow."

"Near as nimble as his father…was, o' course."

"And where *is* Tom?"

"He's down The Blue Bell. Cheers 'im up a bit, having a sup with his friends. Though I could wish he'd remember which roof was his own! Oh, tis not only Tom's accident, Mr Cooper. There's the fall-off in trade. What with the war and then these fancy new fashions. There's no call for stockings nowadays and no profit in socks."

"When I was a youngster, Cathy, " William reminisced, "there was plenty of casual labour to be had, stubbing thistles on the common, clearing thickets, scaring crows. You could sell a live hedgehog for 4d and easily get 2d a dozen for dead sparrows. Everyone had a place in the community: folk pulled together. But that way of life was swept away with the Enclosures. Now it's every man for himself."

A gaggle of children, both her own and her neighbour's, started clamouring around Cathy's knee, whining for the contents of the stockpot and eyeing the visitor with fascinated suspicion. One's boots were mud-caked from hoeing up turnips, another's fingers were red-raw from long stints at yarnwinding, yet another had been sent off as a chimney sweep. *'Suffer the little children…'* William thought, looking into their appealing but not-quite-innocent faces. It was only education and a sound knowledge of the Holy Bible that could wrest them from the trap of grinding toil.

"Cathy, if you and Tom could spare the time to come to service on Sunday, we'd be mighty pleased to see you. You'd learn how the Lord Jesus can undertake for you in your troubles. Meanwhile, I hope you'll accept this," William ended, pushing three florins into her hand.

"Oh, Mr Cooper, sir, I…"

Just then the door was flung open and Henry filled the room with his forbidding presence and shock of fiery hair. "Give it back, Mother! We'll not touch his charity with a bargepole! We ain't on the Parish, yet, Squire."

Cathy turned pale with dismay. "Harry!" she cried. "Hold your tongue, do!"

But Henry was riding and no one could stop him. "We don't want your sort here, bribing us with your dole, thinking you'll get into heaven on the backs of poor folks."

"I can assure you that I glean no pleasure from your hardships. At the chapel, worshippers from all walks of life are welcome."

"Chapel or Church, it makes no odds," snapped Henry. "Parson Morgan deigns to send his curate down here to read the Scriptures and tell us what sinners we are. What do they know? Vicars don't practise what they preach. They're holed up in fine houses, away from real life. A piddling trade, that's all it is."

"Perhaps you are wrong, Harry," William said calmly, "to tar us all with the same brush. The Lord himself did not see eye to eye with the Establishment of his own day. Only taste and see that he is good."

Later, William's intercessions on behalf of young Henry Cart were not brief. Here was an articulate youth, railing against hypocrisy and his own sour conclusions about life. William prayed that they would not slew his thinking any longer.

****

Like Lucifer unleashed for a season, Napoleon broke his fetters and escaped to the Continent where he made a fast and furious bid to rally his disbanded troops. In no time, he had stormed his way towards the Low Countries ready to chance his arm against Gaul's oldest adversary, unconquered since

Norman times and never truly subdued even then.

At Waterloo, a place of little significance apart from the lie of the land which did not favour comers from the south, he engaged the canny Duke of Wellington. The ragged remnants of the British Army, deployed to do battle, was no match for its indoctrinated foe pursuing dreams of *La Gloire*. Returning home after Napoleon's capture a year ago, the soldiers had found themselves hungry and demoralised by lack of work. Their wives and children had forgotten them. They had fought for freedom and no one wanted them. But though God might detest war, it seemed he was on the side of those prepared to withstand a mortal whose overweening arrogance had bled half Europe of its lifeblood over the last two decades. At the eleventh hour, by the merest stroke of fortune, their strength was made perfect and they proved to be victors. The enemy fled in disarray and the mighty, ruthless Emperor was banished to exile on the island of St. Helena for the rest of his days.

The heightened morale of this final triumph was rapidly overtaken by the realities of civilian life. It would be years before the National Debt was paid and the marketplace was humming again. It seemed that, all at once, there was a resurgence of interest in religious faith.

That autumn of 1815 saw a revival at Syston chapel. Attendances were high and a clutch of fresh converts was received into membership. Jonathan Edmondson of the Leicester Circuit, soon to become President of the Methodist Conference, came to preach to the villagers from an upturned ale-barrel on The Green. Casting a glance towards The Pinfold, he was heard to remark that the venue was apt. Against the bleating of stray sheep, his resounding phrases quickened the crowd. *"For by Grace are ye saved through faith; and not of yourselves: it is the gift of God: not of works, lest any man should boast."*

The younger element on the fringes of the gathering who had been indulging in horseplay among themselves, daredevil lads swinging about the oak-tree boughs to impress the lasses, fell silent. Slow though they were to understand, the message intrigued them almost against their will. By the time the preacher had finished, they were convinced that the gospel was for all. In Christ there was neither rich nor poor, neither exalted nor baseborn, neither learned nor ignorant. It was for each to lay down the world's arms, the accepted ways of fighting his corner, and entrust his life to Christ.

Those who wished to dedicate themselves to a new life were then invited by Revd Edmondson to come forward during the singing of a hymn so that he might pronounce a blessing upon them.

Whilst some inner wrestling went on, one or two people shuffled forward. Others took courage from their example and followed. Among them, William Cooper recognised Charles Kemp, an apprentice recently migrated to the Wreake Valley from Northamptonshire whom he was to live to see become a famous lay preacher. But it was the broad-shouldered figure moving determinedly through the press with his head bowed that caused William's gaze to mist. Perhaps only he knew what this day's decision had cost Cathy Cart's firstborn.

"Tell me, Harry," William said afterwards, "what brought about this change of heart?"

"I saw in a flash that fine doings wouldn't get any of us to heaven."

"Indeed, if that were true, only the rich who have time and money would earn their passage. Most are worn down by scratching a living."

"It ain't even enough to live by the Ten Commandments that Parson's so famous for rattling off."

"No one is truly capable of it, that's the rub. The first is the hardest of all to obey."

"But there is one thing we can boast of, Mr Cooper: that Jesus thinks each one of us worth dying for!"

"Pin that to your heart, Harry, and you'll never look back."

With a prayer of thanks, William watched the young man stride homewards beaming with happiness. His very gait bespoke a newfound confidence and yet the aging pilgrim knew that the path, though full of blessings, would be rugged.

And so it proved to be. Though Cathy welcomed the profound transformation in her son, Tom, his father, and William, his brother who worked the loom, tended to distrust it. All this crusading stuff made little sense to them. To place faith in an unseen power was madness which flouted all the laws of nature and commerce. If Henry tried to explain, they taunted and ridiculed him. This radiant new candle in their midst shed light on their own shortcomings and made them prickle unbearably.

After a while, Henry sought to discuss the problem with his mentor, Mr Cooper. "They wanted me to be better tempered, but they can't abide my coming to chapel," he said.

"Pray for them earnestly and bear with them," William advised. "Sometimes we must be prepared to be foolish for Christ's sake."

"But the gospel is all about joy and peace. We're forever at loggerheads at home."

"The Lord also said: 'Not peace, but a sword.' He knows that the love that drives our best endeavours can be an abrasive thing to the world, even to other churchgoers who have not quite grasped the whole truth. Don't you remember, Harry, how you yourself misconstrued my motives before your conversion?"

The lad hung his head. "Yes, sir, I do."

"Well, that is what is meant by 'bearing the Cross.' The world groans under its weight of oppression, but it dare not risk wholesale surrender. It would rather muddle through by itself."

"And a pretty pickle it makes!"

William threw back his head and laughed. "We believers are as prone as any to error, but the difference is that the Lord can use our mistakes to his own good purpose when we commit ourselves in prayer. Just thank God for your deliverance, son, and I will pray that the power of the Spirit enable you to do what you ought."

"The devil of it is," grinned Henry sheepishly, "that both Pa and Will would shine as Christians and put me to shame. They don't gripe and grumble like I used to do!"

"You speak more aptly than you know. Satan will do his utmost to blind them. He is, after all, a fallen angel and very familiar with the truth."

"I reckon it ain't no easy ticket being a Christian."

"You can say that again. But tis the only way to inner peace and healing.

When you're called to suffer, at least you can comprehend why."

****

Whilst the chapel prospered, William's particular delight was the flourishing Sunday School and he began to realise that the small room it occupied behind the main building would need some enlargement. It was his ambition, before his life's work was done, to offer instruction in reading, writing and arithmetic on the premises.

There were days, now, he had to admit, when his energy quickly waned. In cold and windy weather he experienced a raw pain in his chest for which the damp air currents of the Wreake Valley were notorious. But he kept a cheerful countenance and went about his business with as much zeal as ever.

During this period, two sad events took their toll. The first was the death in 1818 of his firmest ally and contemporary, Robert Carr Brackenbury. "I am plunged into melancholy of the darkest tincture," William lamented to an elderly Dr. Ford. "All I have of him is a miniature by an obscure artist and a copy of a drawing of him beside John Wesley's deathbed."

"You have a wealth of memories, my friend, surely more vivid than any picture. And you have your church: a living memorial to his goodness."

The second cause of grief was the demise of the saintly cleric himself in 1820 after a lifetime of shining discipleship. His courage and wit had sustained William at his lowest ebb and pointed the way forward.

Not unnaturally, William began to harbour thoughts of mortality. He lacked the stamina of former days when all-consuming grief would give way to sharpened optimism. It was a cruel paradox that while age brought the wherewithal to cope with disaster, it left behind the shadow of death. It occurred to him that he ought not to delay in making provision for the future of the church. As things stood, he was its temporal owner. John Wesley had foreseen the disadvantages of custodianship and had established a pattern to follow in the trustee system. Accordingly, William called together a group of his friends blessed with sound judgment, long Christian experience and certain fiscal resources. Some had helped to raise the building. There were eleven in all from a variety of trades. Between them they paid the nominal sum of one hundred and thirty pounds for the chapel together with a parcel of land forming part of Whattoffe's House garden.

"The schoolroom will have to be extended," William told Tom Everard, the farmer from Groby. "We must use our facilities to the full. Methodists must play their part in making education available to all."

"Ay, it is the birthright of every Englander. Fee-paying institutions are all very well for those who can afford them and the parish system is sketchy to say the least."

"Without doubt the Church has a duty to enlighten communities. Moral teaching should go hand in hand with the conjugation of verbs and the reciting of tables. Why, our good Dr Ford - may he rest in peace - would use Pythagoras' Theorem as an image of the Trinity!"

Once many obligations had devolved upon the trustees, William felt a certain detachment from the politics of chapel life. Still deeply committed to the practical care of the sick and poor, there was an otherworldly air about him. What he said seemed to resonate in another dimension.

"He's frailer than he admits, Matthew," argued Sarah Dalley. "I don't like that raking cough at all. Yesterday, I heard him in the garden gasping for breath."

"A man who has reached his promised span can't hope to escape the effects of the cursed vapours in this valley, my dear. There's a good measure of vigour in him yet. I daresay his Maker won't be too hasty in claiming him when he can bring young bloods such as William Cart into the fold!"

"He was never the rebel Henry was!"

"Not on the face of it, perhaps, but the fellow had no stomach for any manner of creed."

"They say that Tom sometimes shambles along to the Sunday evening service, blithe as a cuckoo!"

"In no condition to enter the house of God, I'll be bound!"

In the deeper recesses of his heart, William Cooper still entertained the hope that St. Peter's Church, his neighbours' place of worship, would seek a reconciliation with its errant offspring. As time went by, that day seemed further off. The Revd Edward Morgan was denounced by many as a lily-livered time-server who dared not risk offending his Bishop by entering the portals of Dissenters. He was ready to go as far as conducting united prayers in his own schoolroom, but promptly fled to distant climes when called upon to accept a return invitation.

In the town, the lean mean years since the war had loosened the foothold of the archaic Anglican Tory Corporation. Liberal Nonconformists were gaining ground, but changes in the hosiery trade, whom they largely represented, were slow to materialise. Framework knitters like the Carts, who rented their machine from an employer, put up sturdy opposition to the steam power introduced by Thomas Fielding to speed and simplify the process of worsted spinning in manufactories.

"It's a leap in the dark, Mr Cooper," Will Cart told him. "We're on the breadline as it is."

"I can well appreciate your dilemma and I don't have a neat answer," mused his elderly friend with a kind of mystic absorption, "but was embracing the faith not also a leap in the dark?"

This gave the young man food for thought. "If you need some extra muscle putting up that schoolroom, Mr Cooper, me and Harry will do the business. Honest! No gammoning!"

"Then I'll look no further!"

By the end of 1824, the enlargement was complete and the brothers well paid for their services. The smell of fresh plaster and pristine carpentry caused William to sigh with satisfaction as the congregation met for a blessing upon their endeavours. The Dalleys were bidden to share the celebration.

"I can see it all clearly now," William enthused as they sipped tea and nibbled fruit cake after the service. "This will become a seat of learning. We shall go out into the highways and hedgerows and bring the poor and downtrodden to our banquet. We shall hold musical entertainments and lectures, debate topics for mutual instruction. And this is only a modest beginning!"

"Lord love you," chortled Sarah, "that's quite enough to be going on with."

January was bone-achingly cold and William was confined indoors more than he liked, his mind dwelling on scenes from the past. His bouts of consumption sapped the power from his limbs. He suffered from palpitations and wheeziness. Mary Wollett kept the fires well-stoked and plied him with bowls of reviving broth. The Dalleys were dismayed at his blood-stained handkerchieves and Matthew brought round a soothing syrup made from rosemary and opium poppy seeds. "My own patent remedy," the surgeon boasted. "Balm for the membranes."

"I'm exceedingly grateful," William said. He seemed a trifle agitated and bade his neighbour take the fireside chair opposite him. "I've asked Gregson if he'd be good enough to call here in the morning."

"Your friend, the attorney's man? Does he not visit you often?"

"Not in a business capacity, no. Lately, I've been setting my affairs in order, Matt. Some amendments are needed. I wonder, would you do me the great favour of being an executor of my estate?"

"Whatever puts your mind at ease, my friend. But come, we will not speak of this today. I certainly don't intend to watch you sink into a decline."

Matthew Dalley spoke truer than he guessed. William rallied miraculously during the summer. Though he tired easily, he went bustling about the village as if the years had melted away. Only when the November leaves turned to mulch and the damp stench of decay was sharp as salts in his nostrils, did he grow feeble again.

Matthew, on the other hand, a man of robust constitution, who seemed at sixty to have reached the pinnacle of health and status, was taken suddenly in December. He was pouring himself a nightcap of whisky when he clutched his chest and, with an agonised stare, fell in a heap on the carpet, striking his head on the bedpost.

****

"Mary, I have lived too long," William groaned.

"That's no talk for a Christian gentleman, Mr Cooper."

"Maybe not.... but I am weary of this darkling world. The light has gone out upon it."

The devastating loss of his younger neighbour, after thirty years of close confidence and shared adversity, marked the end of an era for the stalwart veteran. By the spring, he was scarcely able to leave his bed.

Matthew's nephew, William Charles Dalley, a very able surgeon, succeeded to the practice next door and his widow and daughter, Mary Ann, took themselves off to a comfortable cottage in the vicinity. Dalley Junior turned out to have as amiable a nature as his uncle and was most attentive to the invalid's welfare, supplying anodyne decoctions and cheerful companionship whenever he could.

"I'm fortunate to have such a likely fellow at my beck and call," William told him.

"It's the least I can do, sir. Uncle Matt used to speak of you in hallowed terms!"

"Nevertheless, as you see, martyrdom does not sit well upon me. Ah lad, my life is near as nothing a closed book."

The months slipped by, the seasons turned and the outside world relinquished its hold. Inescapably, William was drawn into the reality within his own head. Golgotha, he thought. The place of the skull. His opiate slumbers were interspersed with periods of lucid recall, other times and places, other states of being. He remembered the wild freedom of the days long before the Enclosures, recaptured the faces of his mother and father, Abigail, Rob Brackenbury, who each poured half-grasped phrases into his ear throughout that twilight limbo. Half a century had passed since he conceived the notion of building a house to the glory of God. He had defied opposition and brought the Methodist church out of the closet, made it a visible church. His beliefs had turned full circle. Strangely, he found himself falling back on the opinions of his youth: that the true Church of God was not captured in bricks and mortar, nor blocks of ancient granite. It was a living creature.

His voice, by now, was a barely audible rasp. "It is sad, is it not," he observed to John Breedon, his oldest friend from Rotherby, "that what ought to unite mankind is so often a means of dividing it to the death?"

"You have played your part," John assured him. "You have done what your father charged you to do. You have ploughed a straight furrow and sown good seed."

"Water...a sip of water, I beg..."

Several days later, Nicholas Padwick, the curate at St. Peter's, came to administer the Sacrament. William's skin had a translucent pallor but his cheeks were deeply flushed. He seemed in a state of blissful contentment to those of his friends who were present. "Blessed be the Lord. I feel my mind very comfortable," he whispered. "God is love. I know, I feel He is."

"You feel Jesus to be precious to your soul. That is the best testimony of all," said the cleric.

"Glory be to God: I do!"

With that, the servant wedded to his faith slept. His breathing was even, his countenance devoid of all pain and anxiety. A September sundown bloomed on the walls in soft carmine and gold. And now the presences gathered around him, beckoning, not those in the room but the faces of yesterday. In a little while he stirred and opened his mouth a fraction, uttering a single word and finally becoming still.

Some thought he said: "Abba," meaning Heavenly Father. Only John Breedon knew otherwise.

****

They laid him to rest beside his parents among the roots of a venerable beech. Sunshine streamed through its branches like a benison. The mourners at his graveside scattered peaty handfuls of soil and turned to meander along the yew-shadowed paths back to Brook Street for a light repast and the reading of the will.

John Gregson's pleasure at inheriting Whattoffe's House was soon to be marred by uncertainty about its future when a family concern came to a head during the following year.

It was at the annual Hosiers' Dinner held at the Three Crowns Inn in Leicester, which he attended as a guest of the chapel trustee, Will Rawson, that he disclosed his predicament. Rawson had just introduced him to a trade colleague, Mr Thomas Woodcock Needham, with the comment that he fancied his companions had a mutual interest.

"How so?" asked Gregson, seizing the hand of the portly hosier whose flaccid lips were well-stoked with a rotund cigar.

"Why, you have both come into the property of our late friend! Needham's the fellow who snapped up 9, Brook Street when it came on to the market recently. He has already taken up residence there."

"And you must be the owner of Whattoffe's House," Needham deduced, addressing the clerk. "A fine building. Sound order!"

"So I'm given to understand."

"It is remarkable we haven't met before."

"Oh, I haven't made Whattoffe's House my home. It is occupied by tenants. I'm a town man."

Needham's bushy eyebrows shot up in a querying expression. "A capital asset, though. Capital!"

"At the present time, " Gregson confided, "I could wish for assets of a more liquid nature."

Almost as if to grant his wish, Needham plied him with a rummer of porter snatched from the tray of a passing flunky. "Badly dipped, eh?"

"In a manner of speaking, yes. In fact, I am thinking of leaving the district."

"You don't mean to forsake us!" interjected Rawson.

Gregson studied the amber facets of his glass which were like sails full-blown, but he left the beverage untouched. "I believe I must, Rawson. You see, my cousin's mill in Manchester has run into difficulties. He has endured a long spell of sickness and his interests have suffered. If that were not enough, he finds he has been double-crossed by an Egyptian cotton-grower to a quite phenomenal tune."

"Indeed, I had no idea."

"To tell the truth, he has no head for business. He is - how shall I say? - more engaged by the cut and thrust of dealing, the exhilaration of watching vast swathes of percale roll off his looms. Make no mistake, he'll see it done as fast and cheaply as possible, but keep accounts? Regulate his spending? That is not his style at all."

"Then you feel you must shift to help him straighten his affairs?" concluded Needham.

"Or die in the attempt."

"Most commendable, my dear fellow. I own if I had not acted promptly on certain occasions, I should not be enjoying the fruits of my labours today. So you'll be seeking a buyer for Whattoffe's House?"

"Regretfully, yes. It behoves me to find a responsible one, however."

"Look no further, sir! Waste no time with auctioneers and other such extortionists! I'll make you a fair offer! Nay, a generous offer!"

Gregson was on the verge of a reply when Rawson caught him firmly by the elbow and steered him away into the crowd. "Ah! There's Sir Richard! Must introduce you, Gregson. Apologies, Needham! Matters to discuss!"

The bewildered clerk was overcome with an acute embarrassment not unmixed with chagrin. "Why, in the name of heaven, did you do that?" he demanded above the hum of conversation.

"Gregson, I must warn you. Have no truck with that man. I don't say he's downright dishonest, but he's a devoted courtier of mammon. A speculator first and foremost."

"No harm in a modest profit. The Lord himself did not disdain the putting of money to usury. Why, Rawson, you are a man of business. You know the score."

"I make a half-decent living, to be sure. And fill a good many mouths with bread. But there are those," claimed Rawson with a sideways glance, "who rent out their frames without a care for their safety or the high cost of maintenance."

"But a bird in the hand, Rawson! Selling at auction can be a tricky affair. Who can guarantee that the bidding will meet Needham's offer?"

"Truly, I can see the straits you are in, but I wonder you should consider a sale by auction at all. We need a sympathetic purchaser who will undertake to leave the tenants alone. That was our late comrade's earnest wish. As a trustee of the chapel, I cannot neglect their interest."

"You mean that Needham might evict them?"

"If not now, think what a temptation it might prove at some future date when he needs to raise the wind for one of his schemes."

Gregson, for all his thorough attorney's training, felt that his friend was being overcautious. He doubted that Needham would act to invite ill-feeling among the community into which he was settling. On the other hand, he was an employer, a powerful man. Was his air of philanthropy deceiving? "I daresay you have a point," he conceded. "Whattoffe's House has become a refuge for loyal Methodists in need and must remain so."

They obeyed the summons to table where the banquet was laid out before them: saddles of mutton, honey-baked ham and parsnips, stuffed capons and partridges. The trade was evidently not in the doldrums at the moment! Will Rawson reflected that had it not been for these spasmodic booms, he would have been unable to contribute towards the promotion of Methodism in Syston and the building of a grand neo-Palladian chapel in Leicester's Bishop Street. Needham, he noticed, was sinking claret with a will and had tucked his napkin into his collar the minute his rapacious gaze landed upon his dinner. "It is a great pity," Rawson persisted, "that you must relinquish your stewardship so soon. No one could have foreseen your plight, but dear old Will would have been disappointed to see Whattoffe's House pass from your care."

"If only there were an alternative."

"There is another course you might consider," Rawson suggested after a moment's hesitation. "You could mortgage the estate to me at a rate of say…five per cent per annum. That way you will retain ownership."

Instantly, Gregson brightened. "By Jove, what a sharp fellow you are! That is surely the way to keep everyone happy."

"Not quite everyone, I think."

****

That St. Stephen's night, in Brook Street, Syston, the two ladies rose from the supper table to leave their husbands to drink port and broach the arcane topic of trade embargoes.

As Jane Dalley remarked to her hostess, Eleanor Woodcock Needham, the dining-room had undergone a stunning transformation. These days it boasted striped draperies, an elegant mahogany chiffonier, ormolu wall sconces and a carpet of the thickest Kidderminster weave. "Dear Mr Cooper's taste," said Eleanor, "was homely but unrefined."

There had been much talk over the sweetmeats of the King's demise and the accession of his brother, William, Duke of Clarence. George IV, after a lengthy Regency, had succeeded his incurably mad father late in life and had died without heirs, having lost his only daughter and grandchild in childbirth at the tender age of one and twenty. Indeed his sailor brother had no legitimate issue, although half the nation knew that he had spawned a string of bastards by Dorothy Jordan, the mettlesome actress with whom he had set up house in Bushey Park long ago.

"I am inclined to wonder where we're heading," Dalley commented. "A country is only as good as the respect commanded by its monarchy. Honour God, the Church and the Crown, Will Cooper used to say, and all will fall out as it should."

"Fine sentiments in an ideal world, but I'm a pragmatic man myself. The sooner we can dispose of the damned Tory Corporation, the rosier the future will look."

"As an Anglican, you might be expected to side with them."

"As a knitmaster, I cannot. We need better representation. Your average weaver would as soon take an axe to his loom as yield to the changes which would ensure prosperity. And the *laissez-faire* of the Tories encourages them."

"At least you have eggs in other baskets."

"Property's the thing," declared Needham, reaching for the decanter. "Tell me, did you ever hear what became of Gregson?"

"His fortunes are still a trifle shaky, I believe. He has put down roots in the north, though he returns to Leicester occasionally."

"Struck me as something of a greenhorn. He was keen to sell me Whattoffe's House at one time, but suffered a change of heart. I never discovered why."

His neighbour cleared his throat. "It was a most particular bequest. A trust of sorts."

"But he was desperate for funds. I suspected he had no gut for commerce. Small wonder he has not come about!"

"I understand," said Dalley, "that he mortgaged the place to William

Rawson."

"Did he, by Jove!" cried the startled hosier. "How these confounded Methodists hang together!"

"Perhaps it would not have proved a sweet proposition after all, encumbered as it is with three sets of tenants."

"On the contrary," Needham told him, "I should very much have liked to annex the estate."

"There used to be a doorway from your garden into the chapel grounds, you know, but it was sealed up according to Mr Cooper's instructions."

This conjured up an image of exclusion so potent that Needham felt all the anguish of the foolish virgins denied access to the marriage feast for want of lamp-oil.

****

Afterwards, in their own home, the surgeon and his wife discussed the evening over a nightcap of hot chocolate. William was surprised that his neighbour appeared to have taken Gregson's decision as a personal affront. "It seems a touch unreasonable," he said.

"And did you tell him," asked Jane, "that two of the tenants pay no rent and that the third provides an annuity for Mary Wollett?"

"My love, I did not. I did not judge he needed to know."

****

Thomas Woodcock Needham stifled a seismic belch with his napkin after two dishes of devilled kidneys followed by plum duff and custard and picked up the local broadsheet. News of forthcoming elections and demands for reform filled its pages. As was his custom, he sought the Public Notices for assurance that none of his debtors had foundered, then proceeded to the personal columns where his eye was arrested by an entry which gave rise to an almost jubilant cry.

"So Rawson has gone to the great knitting shop in the sky!"

"Where, no doubt," said Eleanor drily, "he is gaining full reward for his charitable deeds."

"Depend upon it." replied her spouse, "there will be an almighty reckoning now!"

But his mind was not running on the heavenly courts of justice.

****

The mills of God and lawyers may grind slowly, but in due course, up in Lancashire, John Gregson received two letters by courtesy of the London - Manchester Mail Coach. One was from William Rawson's executors conveying that his heirs were desirous of a settlement on the mortgage, the other was from Thomas Woodcock Needham with a firm offer for Whattoffe's House 'should you find yourself embarrassed in the wake of the esteemed Rawson's passing.'

He stood gazing into thin air, plunged afresh into the old dilemma. The bowed walls of his modest lodging seemed to bear in upon him. It had been an uphill battle the last four years. His cousin's factory had not long survived the reverses caused by the Alexandrian merchant when new laws were introduced foreshortening the working week. He wondered inconsequentially whether he would be able to procure a slice or two of roast chitterling for his supper.

On the one hand he was loath to part with his inheritance, on the other, here was manna from above. The mortgage had severely taxed his limited income and he was some months in arrears with the repayments. Surprisingly, Needham's offer was not ungenerous and matched favourably, he gauged, the market value.

"The Lord has his own way of doing things," John concluded, "though I don't pretend to know what it is. It would be foolish to fly in the face of providence. I will go at once and speak with this hosier."

Straightaway, he took himself off to the booking office of Mr B. W. Horne and made a reservation to travel on the Peveril of the Peak stagecoach, due to depart at seven the following morning and arrive at The Stag and Pheasant in town some twelve and a half hours later. Feeling cramped and weary, he disembarked at The Halfway House on the turnpike between Loughborough and Leicester and, after a hurried supper, walked the distance to Syston over Lewin's Bridge, across the meadows and past the old watermill.

A half-moon wanly illumined the night between ragged clouds by the time he reached Brook Street and smartly rapped the brass foxhead on Needham's door. It was answered by an elderly womanservant huddled in a shawl who went shuffling off to announce him. In no time, the master materialised and registered an incredulous quirky smile. "Gregson!"

"I…I know that this is an unbridled liberty," faltered the traveller, hat in hand, "but when your letter was forwarded to me by poor Rawson's agent, I felt impelled to discuss the matter face to face."

Scenting an advantage, Needham ushered him into the smoking-room hung with hunting scenes and offered him madeira and sponge drops. "You have come a long way, sir."

"Yes, this very day. And I hope to return by Friday's stage. I have put up at the Rothley inn meanwhile."

"Then we shall hope for a happy issue of this meeting. I take it that the notion of selling your property is not altogether unpalatable to you?"

"I must be candid, sir, It is not what I wish."

"You are not tempted by my rash offer? Damn it, Gregson, the place must be a millstone around your neck!"

"Even so, I feel bound to honour the spirit of the legacy. I cannot hold it lightly that Mr Cooper chose me as its caretaker."

"Caretaker, you say? Is it not a gift to do with as you will?"

Gregson was not a cunning man, but sensed a slight shift in the balance of power. Calmly, he sipped his wine with an air of one prepared to wrestle patiently. "To understand my position, you must first realise that Mr Cooper had a close - some might say paternal - relationship with his tenants."

"Yes, yes," interrupted Needham, "I have heard something of the sort."

"He was aware of their personal circumstances and judged each to deserve the accommodation."

"And you are placed under an obligation to see that they are not disturbed? What a trustworthy fellow you are, to be sure."

"They are not young. They would not easily adapt to a change of environment."

"Indeed, they are not young," echoed the other, stroking his side-whiskers as though lost in calculations of his own. "You seem firmly persuaded I might wish to remove them."

"Forgive me…your eagerness to own the house did appear to indicate that you had a purpose for it."

"Merely that of long term investment. It is a fine dwelling and not so far past its prime that its glory cannot be restored. I know the very people to undertake the thing."

"Not to put too fine a point upon it," pressed Gregson, "were you to find yourself in difficulties at some juncture…"

"I shall not find myself in difficulties!" Needham boomed, seeing the prize slip through his fingers a second time. "I am a man of means! I swear, Gregson, your anxiety to secure the future of these… these… peasants is giving me a headache!"

"Pray, sir, don't put yourself into a passion. I…"

"Am I not a God-fearing citizen who attends the Parish Church each Sunday? You have my word… nay," vowed the hosier, seizing a volume bound in moth-eaten calf from his bookshelf, "I will take my oath upon the Bible that not by one jot or tittle shall their lot be changed!"

Next morning, they convened at a lawyer's office for the signing of the documents. Having achieved his end, Needham presented a cordial front and shook Gregson's hand heartily, wishing him luck with his ventures.

It was not until Gregson was well on his way back to Manchester, riding over misty Saddleworth Moor with a prayer of thanks in his breast, that the acquisitive Systonian discovered that he was to enjoy no revenue from his latest investment.

4

The Wheat and The Tares

1836

The passing of William Cooper, gentleman, marked the end of an era. A whole way of life seemed to vanish with him into the mists of time. Even some of the signposts changed. Town Street was renamed Chapel Street and a little later became the location of another chapel. This was for Baptist worship.

In 1836, a new status was conferred upon Dissenters when they were granted permission to marry in their own chapels.

That same year, the Primitive Methodists, or Ranters, chose to abandon their open air gatherings at Roundhill. They were a steadily growing body who had taken fire from the early Wesleyans but had preferred the atmosphere of camp fire meetings. Locally, they had been inspired by George Handford, a lacemaker from Sileby with an instinctive gift for evangelism. Daniel and Robert Shuttleworth, framesmiths from the same village and trustees of William Cooper's chapel, were well acquainted with him and there was a mixed reaction when the Ranters decided to build their own church in School Street.

Throughout England, change was moving apace. William Wilberforce was putting paid to slavery, a piece of legislation that would have delighted John Wesley since he had been in the vanguard of the abolition movement in the American Colonies. Child labour remained a feature of factory life but hours were reduced and the age of employment pegged at nine. A police force was incorporated to purge the streets of crime and protect honest citizens. Many tariffs were lifted so that there was a freer flow of trade with foreign countries. And Earl Grey's daring Reform Bill of 1832 had left the door to democracy unmistakably ajar when the electoral map was redrawn and wealthier householders were given the vote. Leicester's ailing Tory Corporation breathed its last and a Town Council chosen by ratepayers rose to office.

"The knitters can look forward to a bit o' jam on their crusts," observed Dan Shuttlewood, hailing Will Cart in Turn Again Street. "It bodes well for both of us."

"I wouldn't place a wager on it!" laughed Will. "The trade's had its ups and downs too long. There are no fat profits to be had when half what we earn goes in rent to our masters."

"But didn't I hear you'd taken on another frame?"

"My word, the grapevine twitches! Even so, we can only just keep afloat. There are candles and oil to pay for, to say naught of lost production when a machine breaks down. Still, we owe no man a farthing."

"Bear us in mind when you're in need of servicing and repairs. I'm the best smith this side of the Forest."

Will grinned. "Can't afford the likes of you, Dan. Now my nevvy, John, Harry's youngster, is proving a dab hand at fixing minor faults. Maybe you should give him some indentures and teach him a thing or two. He's a good lad, attends the Sunday School regular."

Humble Henry Cart, now a husband and father, had been deeply touched by a bequest of two gold guineas from his saintly hero, Mr Cooper. His skills as a wool-comber had been forsaken for a steadier income as a hairdresser and he thanked God that, though poverty might lurk around the corner, it was a shackled enemy.

Shortly after his brother's conversation with Daniel Shuttlewood, he received a visit from the framesmith in respect of young John who might be seeking an apprenticeship.

"I hear he's a nifty rascal," said Shuttlewood mischievously.

"Ay, he's as sharp as needles. Always needs to be doing with his hands. I'd be mighty glad for you to get him trained up."

"And what say you, Cart Junior?" asked Shuttlewood, catching the lad by the ear.

The smirched face winced and reddened with pain, but the mirthful eyes shone with spirit. "I'd say you'd get the best of the deal, mister!"

They fell to gossiping as artisans will and Shuttlewood mentioned the meeting of chapel trustees which had taken place the night before. "We were sore dismayed to hear that Squire Needham has bought Whattoffe's House."

"It's never changed hands? I'd not a blind notion it was for sale."

"Nor had we, that's what nettles. Appears it was all tied up with Old Rawson's estate."

"But what of the Ormes and the other folk who live there?"

"The Squire's given his solemn assurance they'll not be turned out. But tis a sad day for Methodists, old Mr Cooper's place gone for good."

Henry Cart shook his head. "If we'd known, we could have called a prayer meeting, committed the problem to the Lord, for I'm blessed if I can see how we'd have pooled enough dough to buy it ourselves."

****

Scarcely had the damsel Queen Victoria ascended her late Uncle's throne, than the steam age came roaring into the lives of provincial people. The Midland Counties Railway linking Leicester with Derby was opened in 1840 and was further connected with Peterborough in 1848. Thomas Cook was busy organising day excursions from Leicester to Loughborough and, before long, the little station at Syston was fairly buzzing with passengers eager for a taste of adventure to brighten their humdrum lives. They were beginning to find a spare shilling or two in their pockets for such delights.

In 1842, the Wesleyan chapel was enlarged and renovated and the Georgian arched window and vestibule moved to the side. In addition, the schoolroom was demolished to make way for a bigger one. Five years later, under the supervision of Samuel Driver, William Bennett, Edward Kirk and young John Cart, the Sunday School comprised one hundred scholars governed by twenty teachers. There were two per class, each on duty at both sessions on alternate Sundays. Soon a rota was drawn up so that reading and writing could be taught on Monday evenings.

"I only hope," said John Cart, casting his eyes up to heaven, "that Mr Cooper can see the harvest we're reaping from his labours."

"Ay, lad," agreed William Bennett, "I mind him often. D'you know, I were just a flax-dresser when the old boy died - you'd be no more'n a nipper - but he left me summat as changed my life. Five shining sovereigns all at once in my hand, just like my nag'd romped home at Leicester Races! Billy Bennett, I says to myself, these are talents from the Lord. Use 'em wisely. So I went out and bought a patch of meadow and a goat and a pig by and by..."

"Now you're a farmer in grand way of business!"

"That's not all, lad. Now I give a tithe to the Lord and feed his lambs."

****

If the watchword was 'progress' during this tumultuous period, it did not always go hand in hand with prosperity. Whereas the dynasts of cottonmills, iron foundries and shipyards were developing their skills in leaps and bounds, the slim profits earned by the knitmasters made the cost of mechanisation prohibitive. Stuck in a vicious bind, the workers attempted to form trade unions and embarked on a series of fruitless strikes which did away with hundreds of jobs and placed a strain on the rates. The New Poor Law was nowhere near adequate and the late forties saw a rise in the numbers begging on the streets of Leicester. Siberian winters dealt a raw edge to their privations and further elevated the price of bread. It was only to be expected that there would be a steady erosion of the hosiery labour force beckoned by the johnny-come-lateles of the boot and shoe industries.

In the light of this, Thomas Woodcock Needham resolved to pursue a policy of retrenchment. He awoke one morning to an opaque feathering of frost on his windowpanes and realised he could no longer see his way clear to further expansion. He was fifty-two and felt that he should have been at the peak of his powers.

That afternoon, he escorted Eleanor in her best poke bonnet to a Splendid Exhibition of the Arts at the Theatre Royal, Horsefair Street, Leicester which had been turned into an assembly room for the purpose. It was a spectacular show which the county was flocking to see. Such delicious diversions as firework displays, tableaux and an automaton on a slack wire were not to be resisted. On the Gallery staircase, they ran into George Angrave, hosier, who appeared to be squiring a party of excited females.

"Mixed bag of relations," he said by way of introduction. "Threatened to hide the key to my liquor cupboard if I didn't bring 'em along." Gloomily, Angrave contemplated the prospect of a dry future and decided he had narrowly gained the better part of the bargain.

"Eleanor, my dear," Needham turned to his wife, "if you were to mingle with the ladies, trade the latest gossip, that sort of thing, we yokefellows might retreat to the smoking room for a short while. What do you say?"

Eleanor looked less than pleased but did as she was bidden. Angrave brightened and went so far as to proclaim his gratitude for the reprieve.

The men settled among the plush chesterfields and winged chairs of the saloon and inevitably fell to discussing affairs of the loom. "Hard times, eh Squire?" said Angrave, delving into his pocket for an ivory snuff box.

"Damned Chartists and Radicals have made a poor fist of things, stirring up the barbarians in the name of social reform. If they're not running riot, they're on strike!"

"Oh, we've seen the last of them in the town, take it from me, Squire. Forever quarrelling among themselves. The dust will settle soon enough."

"The mischief is already done! The cry for higher wages won't be stifled in a hurry," grumbled Needham. "How those tub-thumping Dissenters strive to prick the nation's conscience!"

"You, sir, I perceive, are very much of the rich-man-in-his-castle, poor-man-at-his-gate school."

"It is to be preferred to the present unholy order of things."

"Come now," begged his affable companion, offering snuff from a finely chiselled box, "surely the church has a duty to take up the cudgels on behalf of the poor."

Needham craftily pressed a coat-button between his thumb and forefinger in order to trap a fuller pinch of the blend. "The poor are ever with us," he snorted. "The church has no business meddling in politics. Oh, I have flirted with the ideology of the Wesleyan brethren - it is all very noble and worthy - but it does not reckon with human nature."

"It preaches Christ crucified alongside its good works."

"It might do better to recognise that an unbroken horse is apt to throw its rider with sometimes fatal consequences. I tell you, Angrave, I have not the money to meet the demand for better rates of pay. As it is, I must cut back, trim the fat, sell off assets. Whattoffe's House will be the first thing to go!"

An image of the sealed doorway reared up in Needham's mind. The property had yielded no satisfaction and he had long lost the desire to gamble upon restoration. For some obscure reason, he felt that the chapel formed a mystic barrier between himself and the fullness of possession. This was only in part explained by the constraints laid upon him for, by now, Mary Wollett and all the original tenants, save one widow, had died and he was able to demand a suitable rent for two of the cottages. If the chapel were to fall into disuse, however, the house with its own native garden would have been a premier site for development. In other places, Methodism had waxed and waned: in Syston, it appeared to have taken firm root.

Angrave's eyes glinted with sharpened interest. For his sins, he had lately been appointed a trustee of the chapel, having a familial interest in its concerns. "You mean to put William Cooper's old place on the market?"

"I have no option."

"You'll approach the Wesleyans, naturally, Squire?"

"I'll do no such thing! It shall go at auction to the highest bidder. Anyway, who among them can afford to fly so high?"

"A wealthy almsgiver, perhaps, looking for a righteous cause," suggested Angrave. "Their supporters come from far and wide."

"Ah, debts of conscience," riposted Needham. "I believe the Almighty's coffers resound with offerings from those anxious to buy a passage to heaven!"

A HOUSE NOT MADE WITH HANDS

****

Within the space of two days, the kitchen at Bourdon Farm, William Bennett's abode, was buzzing with the news. George Angrave had been in touch with Daniel Shuttlewood and a hasty meeting of chapel dignitaries had been arranged over mugs of tea, spiced muffins and lardy cake. A liberally-stoked fire burned merrily and shot sparks on to a faded rag rug whilst a hoist-up laundry rack festooned with smocks and unmentionables steamed gently against the cracked ceiling.

They put their heads together around the rough deal table. "If the Lord be for us, who can stand against us?" pronounced Angrave for the chair. "Gentlemen, here's a God-given chance to regain Whattoffe's House for the benefit of those it was intended for."

"Hear, hear," seconded Samuel Driver. "We owe you a vote of thanks, George, for calling this meeting so speedily and to Bill for the use of his kitchen."

"What about his Missus," piped up John Cart, scoffing a third sample from her oven.

They all agreed that the farmer's wife had been unstinting with the victuals and that the cook's art was second only to the miracle of the loaves and fishes. This done, they settled down to the matter in hand.

"A good thing George ran into the Squire in town," remarked Shuttlewood.

"He wouldn't know you was an offshoot of the Cooper family," submitted Henry Cart to the chairman. "A Zion of the dynasty, so to speak."

"I'll bet he never!" said John, licking his fingers.

"Scion," corrected Driver. "Good grief, he's not the Holy City, just a sprig from the sticks!"

"Same difference," shrugged the elder Cart. "Anyhow, old Will's got no aftercomers of his own, so it's up to us to see him right. I back we call a prayer meeting."

The general consensus was that petitioning the Heavenly Father would be a wise move but that further measures were needed as earnest of their intent. The celestial platter was, after all, currently piled with the problems of the poor and sick, to say nothing of the Monday night reading and writing classes. "If tis his will," maintained Farmer Bennett, "he'll contrive a way."

The framesmith from Sileby, a hammer and nails man, nevertheless drew their attention to an acute lack of spondulicks. There was a limit to how many high teas and concerts could be put on at short notice, the pianoforte needed tuning and there was a shortage of benches in the Sunday School. "Where's it coming from, tell me that? It takes every mite we have to keep our present premises up to scratch."

"And do our work in the parish," added Driver.

"Which brings us neatly to a fact we are, perhaps, overlooking," Angrave stated. "We have cast not a little bread upon the waters over the years. This community has good reason to be grateful to Methodists for improving its life. Why don't we get up a subscription? Appeal to the goodwill of Syston people?"

A moment's reflection was broken by bumbling noises of assent. The meeting was ready to adopt the idea.

"We shall pray continually, in church and out of church," declared Angrave, "and we shall see whether our better deeds come up as a remembrance before the Lord."

****

For no apparent reason, the landlord of the School Street tenements neglected to put them up for sale during the whole of that summer. Henry Cart was of the strong opinion that it was a direct result of the prayer meeting, for it gave the chapel committee a welcome space to canvas aid.

The campaign ran less than smoothly. Happily, a large number of people were well-disposed towards the sect but penury was rife and the Anglican Church a drain upon their wages. Although Dissenters had earned most political rights, every householder was obliged by law to pay rates levied by the Parish Vestry and any brave rebel who made it a point of principle to refuse was summarily clapped into jail. Bill Bennett was a Nonconformist representative of this body and had a particularly invidious task in appealing to villagers on behalf of the Methodists. The Church, like a great wounded beast impeding the pack, was despised by all who were not part of it. Parson Morgan had failed to advance the cause of ecumenism in half a century.

"What does he do?" demanded Bennett, "whenever we ask him down to t'chapel? Why, he ups with his carpetbag and goes gallivanting off to the Continent! More brass than brain!"

"The Rector's fortunate that Mr Gregg from Brooksby will carry his burden of duty when he's missing," said Samuel Driver. "It could work in our favour, though, Bill."

"How's that?"

"Methodists will be seen as reliable persons who don't quit their post when it suits them. While we're seeking funds, we'll trawl for more scholars and members, acquaint the humble and downtrodden with our creed."

The notion deeply inspired John Cart. "We'll beard the fray, carrying neither purse nor scrip, just as the first disciples did."

Samuel Driver judged right when he spoke of the wisdom of challenging simple folk for, so elastic were the resources of those whose lives became dedicated to the Lord, that out of their poverty they pledged more than those who had much. Money was a hedge against the harsh winds of reality and the craving for a faith among those who possessed it, less ardent. A scattering of souls, young and old, were recruited to attend worship. Some believed that Methodism was the force to stamp out social injustice and wanted a stake in New Jerusalem. Others needed a personal anchor. A wretched few had wills stiffened by hardship: they struggled bitterly and cursed the dawning of the day. But the careworn majority were startled to learn that a loving Saviour had died for them. They had viewed religion as a luxury - good for the franchised and the fanatic.

"Time and again, as I stand on those cottage doorsteps listening to weary mothers with infants lodged on their hips," glowered Driver, "I hear how fine ladies gather up their skirts and shift along their pews when the poor are bold enough to go to Mass."

"It makes me wonder who needs our ministry more," mused Angrave wryly.

"Many labourers stay in bed on Sunday because they don't get enough sustenance," reported John Cart.

"A quarryman told me he never rose on the Sabbath because it was the only chance his wife had to wash his body-linen," added his father.

It was a tough assignment but, by and by, the list of subscribers lengthened. As they went about their business, chapel members aroused the interest of everyone they met. There was Pryor, the cattle dealer, Ardron the farmer, Radford, the butcher, Tookey, the coal merchant, Underwood, the shoemaker. From the town, there was Boyer, the gentleman of leisure, Fowkes, the grocer, Hughes of the same trade, Wilde, the druggist.

By the end of November, when the bills advertising the auction of Whattoffe's House were posted, a wealth of support had been amassed.

"We have smitten the living fountain from the rock," said Driver. "Even as a missionary venture, we have cause to rejoice."

****

The man in the wide-awake hat and darned coat paused in the taproom doorway of the Midland Counties Arms Hotel to stamp the snow from his boots. His sharp black eyes were full of whimsy as he took in the scene.

Flames as long as posthorns raced up the chimney and the bottle-glass windows were blind with steam. The babbling din faltered. A dozen pairs of questioning eyes settled upon the stranger, but no one hailed him. He strode confidently towards the bar, making a swathe through the atmosphere thick with smoke from pine and pipe, and demanded pigeon pie, boiled potatoes and a jar of the local bitter.

Farmer Bennett, having done his apple turnover full justice, shrugged and picked a clove-stalk from between his teeth. It was a staggering turnout for Messrs Holland, Warner & Sheppard's auction sale. He trusted the Good Lord knew his oats and that the attention of speculators would be diverted from Lot No. 3 in which he himself had so fervent an interest. He was there on behalf of the chapel trustees to bid for the house now in alien hands. At five minutes to two, just as the proceedings were about to begin, he was heartened to see George Angrave step into the saloon, brushing snow from his greatcoat.

"Keen as mustard, this crowd," grunted Bennett.

"Have faith, man! I daresay half of them are taking refuge from the snowstorm."

"I don't see the Squire."

"He's holding forth in the Snug. Caught a glimpse of him on my way in."

As if on cue, Needham sauntered into the room, replete on the best fare of the house, and indulged in some jocular repartee with old Cabby Hubbard who had defied the snow on crutches rather than miss the goings-on. The hosier stationed himself in a corner, well back from the auctioneer's desk, exuding an air of complacency. Lots 1 and 2 were summarily disposed of and Bennett braced himself to do battle.

The desired lot was introduced and amply described. His throat felt parched and his tongue swollen. A panting engine towing coal-wagons screamed and clattered through the nearby station. Silence fell so that the audience had to be cajoled into an appreciation of its fortune. After such a panegyric, only the dark newcomer was bold enough to offer a startling fifty guineas to a chorus of whistles. Then, cautiously, the bidding began to jump to and fro, catching like sparks among the throng, until only three contenders remained. They were Bennett, Simeon Applebee, a Leicester schoolmaster, and the mysterious figure in the felt hat who appeared to be acquainted with no one.

In leaps of five pounds, the bidding spiralled. Bennett mopped the moisture from his brow. He was beginning to lose his nerve for he was reluctant to commit the chapel to a debt the pledges would never cover and the extent of essential repairs had yet to be fully assessed. In great anxiety, he turned to his companion. "Best quit," he hissed.

"Press on!"

Just then, Angrave caught the sly satisfaction on Needham's countenance. One hundred and sixty. And five. One hundred and seventy. And five. One hundred and eighty pounds, gentlemen…"

"Nay, that's enough! Best let it be. If Him Above had meant us to have it, he'd a gi'n us a few extra bob!"

"An awful pity," muttered Angrave, "for tis my belief that foreign-looking fellow is an agent of Needham's, planted to up the bidding. See how their eyes communicate!"

"You mean he's not a *bona fide* customer?"

"I'd stake my life on it. Unless I'm mistaken, he'll gauge exactly when to withdraw."

And so he did. Whattoffe's House was finally knocked down to Mr Applebee for the sum of two hundred and ten pounds which many agreed was excessive. By all accounts it was to become a boarding school for the sons of gentlefolk who sought a scientific and classical education.

Bennett looked crestfallen as the tension drained away. A wave of bitter disappointment overtook him. He shuffled the peak of the cloth cap he always wore for going to market back and forth through his fingers. Divine plan or otherwise, he realised how desperately bent he had been on winning the prize. "Hell and tarnation! Beggin' your pardon, Mr Angrave, sir. That knave was lining his pockets all along. He done it to put our nose out of joint, I swear!"

"He did it to obtain maximum profit."

"Them high and mighty Anglicans think they can ride roughshod over sinners like us. Twere an ill day when that vulture got his talons on Will Cooper's bequest."

"Bill, give over fretting. It was not meant to be."

"But we'd have put it to good use and looked after the poor. Instead of that, it's to be a place where young toffs will learn the trick of trampling them down."

"You were all for quitting a little earlier. All for giving God a hand in the affair."

"Nay, but I nivver guessed we were being double-crossed, Mr Angrave,"

"Should that make a difference, I wonder?"

The farmer ground his teeth sullenly, his usual bright goodwill gone. "You may go to the cattlemarket and judge a beast by his head, his rump, his shanks, but man is a pig in a poke." He unhooked a weathered mantle from the cloakstand, catching his own distorted reflection in the badly silvered mirror. "There's no telling what manner of breed lives under his hide!"

"The pathways of the human heart are rarely straight and true. I fancy there is much to be learned from this day's affairs."

****

There was a pressing need to renew the Trust.

The Wesleyans were entering the second half of the century and no amendments had been made since William Cooper's day. Only three out of the eleven original trustees remained and members had been haphazardly co-opted to fill the breach without any well-defined commitment to the role.

"We have allowed our responsibilities to slip," said George Angrave. "Before the year is out, we must set about forming a new committee."

Everyone knew he was right, but his haranguing tone caused hackles to rise. Richard Boyer and the two Shuttlewoods had served faithfully since 1818 and others had either been dragooned into service or had unstintingly devoted themselves to good works over the years. Angrave, a relative latecomer, had surfaced as a result of his natural flair for organisation.

The fate of Whattoffe's House had plunged them all into dejection, none more so than Angrave himself who was the Coopers' kith and kin. They had intended to use their founder's house for charitable purposes and had been confident they could count on the Lord to strengthen their arm. Although, as Pryor, the cattle dealer, pointed out: worse destinies might have befallen the Cooper heritage.

"That's as may be," argued Radford, the butcher, "but an Anglican school for privileged brats is no help to the starving."

"Even well-heeled Nonconformists would hesitate to send their sons to such an institution," maintained Ardron, the farmer.

"That is why in Leicester," said Boyer, the gentleman of means, "chapel-goers strive to acquire their own academies, but it is not easy to make them pay. You'll recall the Proprietory School in New Walk lasted only a decade."

At this, Angrave lost his temper. "The everlasting rivalry between Church and Dissent is a grievous scourge!" he stormed. "These are supposedly enlightened times. How can we be brothers in Christ and evangelise society if we are constantly at war? Though it condemned him, Wesley did not teach us to despise the established church."

"Fine talk," grumbled the down-to-earth Bennett, still sore at the outcome of the auction, "but your head's full of fleece if you fancy things can be changed overnight. Blatherin' Pharisees with their incense and images have allus looked askance at chapel flock. Why, the Church is nobbut English popery!"

Angrave's steel-grey eyes blazed. "Nonsense, Billy! You'd do well to remember that the early Methodists were taken for Papists!"

"Papists or not," shouted Tookey, the coal merchant, picking furiously at the grime under his fingernails, "I'm damned if I'll render my hard-earnt brass unto Caesar with a cheerful heart!"

A prickly silence ensued until Boyer retrieved the situation. "Come, come, gentlemen, it will be said that not for nothing are we called Dissenters!"

"There is too much readiness to cast stones all round," Angrave agreed. "Why, I myself must confess that I cannot be absolutely certain Needham tinkered with the bidding last week. Either way, it makes no odds, for the Lord did not see fit to return Whattoffe's House to us."

"Perhaps," Boyer was bold to suggest, "we ought to set about putting our present house in order before we can expect to gain another."

****

Simeon Applebee sat at his desk with his head between his hands. Beyond the window, the street shone bluish white with vestal snow, but he was dully aware of the approach of trampling beast and cart.

"I wanted it for your mother's sake," he said brokenly. "A temple of learning to her memory. It would have eased the pain of loss."

The pale youth with fledgling beard and scarified locks who hovered on the hearthrug was stricken with a pang of something akin to remorse. "The fellows at the Club might wait a little longer, Pa. They cannot dun me for a debt of honour."

"Hold your peace, lout! Can you be flesh and blood of mine to utter such sentiments? You may strip a man of wealth and raiment, you may strip him of his dignity, but whilst honour remains, he is a king. A man without honour deserves to starve in the gutter!"

"Twas mere sport, Pa. An innocent diversion…"

"Innocent! You call gaming innocent when a man might stake his very existence on a hand of cards? Time was when this town was sober and respectable, but these woolly-minded Liberals have let in the devil with democracy that they should boast an accursed casino as one of its amenities."

"Then what is to be done?"

"What is to be done? I'll tell you what is to be done, Edward," declared Simeon, rising and pacing the room with an air of purpose. "See this? It is a draft upon my banker for Whattoffe's House. I shall tear it to shreds and write others to your creditors, not to condone your lust for excess, but to redeem the family name, and you may have it on your conscience to the grave that your mother was denied her dying wish."

****

Thomas Woodcock Needham drained a good three inches of neat scotch from his glass in the hope of effecting a swift recovery from apoplexy. "No!" he stated emphatically to his agent. "No, I shall not be putting the property up for auction a second time. It must go to the underbidder. I need funds *now*."

"So it shall go to the Methodists for the sum of one hundred and eighty pounds?"

"That's what I said, Holland. I dare swear it is an answer to all their supplications and there will be rejoicing in heaven this very hour. I am too wise a man to tilt with the Creator. I know when I am beat!"

****

Thus, in the year of the Great Exhibition, when Britain was confidently displaying her wares and technology to the world and just before the men of the Wreake Valley became embroiled in the far-flung squabbles of Eastern

Europe and the Crimea, the spirit of William Cooper's bequest to posterity was fulfilled.

5

The Harvest

1886

"Indeed, Miss Underwood, our choir does you credit. Its members have performed with singular energy."

The Revd Joseph Westcombe surveyed the packed schoolroom in which three or four score widowed parishioners had gathered to enjoy a cold beef salad and spiced muffins followed by a festive entertainment of words and music.

Humbly, the shoemaker's daughter owned that the success of the evening was due in no small measure to the enthusiasm of her choristers who bore out the best traditions of their creed.

"Yes, our Wesleyan heritage was born in song," agreed the minister.

"It does the heart good to see such a happy assembly," observed John Rodgers, his father-in-law, who had returned to his native district after a long absence during a youth spent with his grandfather at Inkersall in Derbyshire.

John Cart, whose idea the occasion had been, grinned with modest pleasure. He was on the threshold of retirement now, deep refts of myopia smocking his brow from half a century of tending and mending stocking frames. After the boom of the sixties, when Thomas Woodcock Needham had last drawn breath, the industry was at its lowest ebb and unemployment was swelling the demand for bread tickets. He was keen that the chapel should play a key part in alleviating distress. "Tis passing strange," he reflected, his fervid grey eyes bright as buttons, "that we are on the eve of Her Majesty's Golden Jubilee, a nation which is pleased to call itself 'the workshop of the world' and still I see evidence of as great a poverty as I ever witnessed."

"Ay, John, the poor are always with us," sighed the minister, "but inasmuch as we have done it unto these, we have done it unto Christ."

"A sobering notion, Mr Westcombe, when you think on it. We've no leave to go congratulating ourselves yet. Why, we should want a hall twice this size to begin our duty!"

"Not only that," Agnes Underwood reminded them, "we need a larger church. Though our membership stands at some fifty-two persons, many more come to worship through our good works in the village."

John Rodgers wholeheartedly agreed. "We are one of the older societies. The twentieth century is on our doorstep and we have made no provision for it."

Black Underwood, shoemaker, warmed to the theme. Having enjoyed a long association with the Sunday School, it was the welfare of the children which concerned him. "The young 'uns spoil for mischief when they're herded too close together."

The group had been joined by Vincent Moore, a somewhat pompous commercial traveller wearing pebble spectacles. From time to time, he was called upon to contribute articles to the *Wesleyan Methodist Messenger* as well as undertaking various secretarial duties. "And we must not neglect our Mutual Improvement Society. We have discussed Socialism and the character of Oliver Cromwell. We have studied geology, the travels of Stanley and the lives of great men, all topics which appeal to those with an intellectual leaning. Our number increases apace and is drawn from those who might otherwise not attend our Sabbath services."

Mr Westcombe listened intently, as though focused on an inner horizon. It had often struck him that the Georgian lineaments of the chapel were too crude and basic for his own empire-building generation. The country had come a long way since those wayward days. People were informed and tastes more sophisticated. There was much to be said for the Gothic tradition so powerfully rendered in modern architecture, gracing the lawcourt, the railway station and the municipal office. Nonconformists had no place for the ornamentation of Rome, but an airy, no-nonsense edifice with a lance-shaped arch or two above its portals would look very well indeed. "It would be a betrayal of our founders not to move with the times," he said, "although how we shall accomplish the task before us, God only knows."

"Happen we ought to raise the matter with the trustees," Black suggested.

"My friend," promised the cleric, "I will see that it is put on the next agenda."

****

By the time the meeting was convened in the early part of Jubilee year, Joseph Westcombe had allowed his enthusiasm to run away with him. He was midway through a three year term of office and was unlikely to see any major endeavour accomplished. If his ministry proved popular and he himself did not feel called elsewhere, the committee would elect to retain him for a further period. Though he was a staunch believer in the Methodist system, the peripatetic rootlessness of its clergy sometimes dismayed him. The best he could hope for was to be the instigator of a splendidly daring venture.

He was totally unprepared, therefore, for the wall of opposition which met his proposal. It was both frustrating and bewildering that in the climate of the debating chamber, even those who had pressed for the initiative had lost some of their fervour.

"We shall be in debt till doomsday," complained Manahath Cart, John's relation who shared the same mechanical skills.

"A millstone around our necks for years," endorsed Bill Nichols, the ropemaker.

"It would be the height of folly to take such a risk," agreed Henry Gibbs, the merchant.

"The poor must first be fed," insisted Charles Mason, the grocer. "The church is more than four walls and an altar."

"There's something in that," said John Cart, "but a larger building would be an asset to the whole community, well-off and poor alike."

"Gentlemen," the pacific Rodgers addressed them from the chair, "bear in mind that as professing Christians, we are not alone. We do not act in our own strength. The Lord will respect our desire to further his Kingdom, if indeed that desire be honest."

"I daresay we should be entitled to a connexional grant," said the minister. "That would provide the impetus we seek even if it is not immediately forthcoming."

"It is our duty to prepare a way forward," continued his father-in-law.

"Ay, we've to invest in the rising generation," added Black Underwood, "no two ways about it."

The prospect of an orgy of fund-raising loomed like a nightmare to the more sober faction who stiffened their argument.

"The Lord gave us common sense to use," grumbled Manahath Cart.

"Didn't he exhort us to be good stewards of our gifts?" demanded Henry Gibbs.

The minister was quick to remind them, via the Parable of the Talents, that sound stewardship did not consist in hoarding one's assets. "To hide a gift is to lose it," he averred. "There were harsh words for the servant who look no risks. The point is, my friends, that faith takes over where reason leaves off."

The merchant, the ropemaker, the grocer and one of the framesmiths were of a mind in thinking the clergyman overly idealistic. He was still a young man and had a long way to go. Needed to see a bit of life, find out how the real world ticked. They were every bit as concerned about the future of the church as he was, but sometimes it was necessary to consolidate.

"I fear that I have lost them," mused Mr Westcombe sadly, after the meeting. "They will not easily bend."

"Give it time, Joseph. Give it time," said John Rodgers consolingly. "We must pray for a positive outcome."

"They talk about the Scots and the dalesfolk of the north, but East Midlanders are equally inclined to keep a tight rein on their purse strings."

"They fear to seek charity in the trough of a recession."

"Yes, I do see. But bread alone will not suffice. We have it on the best authority."

Rodgers let go a profound sigh. "It's the age-old conundrum," he said. "In the end a man is ruled by either banker or bishop."

Westcombe cast his wife's parent a look of concern, noting his sudden grey and dejected aspect. Sometimes he would wince from waves of griping pain around his midriff, though he seldom acknowledged it. He was not yet elderly, but there were moments when the shadow of mortality lay heavily across him.

When the meeting closed, some of the trustees repaired to Manahath Cart's lodgings to brew tea and a consume a handsome supper of Stilton cheese, granary bread and pickles. They ambled through the gaslit streets, deep in a conversation which had a vaguely minatory tone. Syston was expanding. It boasted well over eighty tradesmen and a growing body of professionals. The straggling clusters of cottages were now overshadowed by the townhouses of people of substance and tended to reflect the dips and peaks of the local economy. Urchins in patched breeches and cramping hand-me-down shoes stoned pigeons for food whilst the sons of gentlemen would return from private tuition in glossy calf buttonboots and serge suits to tables bearing prime hams and apple dumplings.

"Makes no sense to throw good money away on bricks and mortar when half the village is on the breadline," said the plump grocer, shaking his head.

There were murmurs of assent all round. Only John Cart was silent. He was thinking of a certain alabaster jar of precious oil of spikenard which, in the Lord's day, some grumbled, might have been sold for three hundred pence and given to the poor.

****

On June 21st of that year, 1887, the Queen celebrated her Golden Jubilee and travelled in resplendent style from Buckingham Palace to Westminster Abbey where a Thanksgiving Service was held in the company of sumptuously attired Indian princes and ambassadors from every civilised nation on earth. A vast necklace of beacons was lit from Land's End to the Shetland Isles and the laird dined with the crofter, the lord with the labourer, the squire with the shopkeeper, rich and poor, old and young, all bowed heads as one for the Grace, and strife was forgotten.

The weeks which followed saw a mighty display of Britain's defences. There was a review of the Army at Aldershot, of her Majesty's Volunteers at Buckingham Palace, of the Fleet at Spithead.

The Empire, it seemed, was intact. The nation could sleep soundly.

At the manse, the Revd Joseph Westcombe crafted a masterly address about the perils of gathering into barns where moth and rust corrupt. "The leading edge of faith is always hazardous," he concluded, "but that is the very ground which yields the firmest foothold."

****

Fourteen months later, in the middle of August, he packed his trunks and delivered his last testimony in Syston. He had been recognised as a tower of strength to the Mutual Improvement Class, his congregations had been sizable and, it was noted, there had been the greatest increase in the quarterly collections for eight years. In the parish, he had been the champion of all creeds and classes and his going was felt to be a loss to the whole area.

This notwithstanding, he knew that he had failed to initiate a renewal of faith. Plans for the new church building were no further forward. His arguments had been resisted and it was with no small sorrow that the ailing John Rodgers saw his beloved Binnie prepare to take off alongside her husband for more fertile pastures.

"It is a premature departure," he told Albinia, his wife. "A further spell in office and he would have brought them round. I earnestly hope the brethren in Doncaster deserve him."

Scarcely had the dust settled from the tilbury which transported the Westcombes to the station, than plans went ahead for the Reception Meeting to greet the incoming cleric. The Wesleyan wives turned their hand to baking rich fruit cakes, raised pies and gooseberry jellies for the grand tea which was to precede a service in chapel.

Tom Borderick's son, Nathan, a brawny lad of thirteen, was co-opted to set up trestle tables and carry in towering stacks of crockery. That summer he had gleefully wished his schooldays farewell and started a job as a 'bricky'. He took great pride in trimming a trowel of mortar to bond each rust-red row.

Lilian Stevenson, the corn merchant's wife, humped in the freshly scoured and burnished tea urn, fretting because no one remembered asking the guests to bring their own knives and forks. In a far corner, a village veteran, huddled in a shawl, presided from her Bath chair. This was Mary Charlesworth, Lilian's grandmother. She was accustomed to let drop salty pearls of wisdom on feast days and fast days, her bright eyes darting everywhere. If the flesh was frail, the spirit was keen.

Mary had been born a Cart, one of Tom and Cathy's brood, and was a great aunt to the maturing generation of John and Manahath's children and great grandmother to Lilian's youngster, Robert. Her fond boast was that she was the same age as the century and, despite the Queen's long reign, had been the loyal subject of four different monarchs. When she was a slip of a girl, King George III had finally lost his wits. She was just three when William Cooper's gem of a chapel had been dedicated and could well recall the accents of pride and reverence with which her family had spoken of the old gentleman. Now some were saying that the building would not do, others that it would have to do. In olden times, opinion had been unanimous within the sect. Now, when it no longer suffered persecution, the followers were often divided among themselves. Prayer and faith, it seemed, were in danger of becoming casualties of the drive to conquer poverty and intemperance. "The poor have a right to be educated," she would say. "They deserve a chance to stand on their own two feet." Though, she had to admit, that this often meant the young folks detaching from their roots. Take her great nephew, John Henry Cart… His father, John, and grandfather, Henry, had been content to be the rough diamonds of the parish, but John Henry had done so well with his architect studies that he had got himself hitched to Sam Driver's posh granddaughter and cleared off to London where he had managed to get elected Mayor of East Ham! "Cart name's not good enough for his fancy friends," scorned the old lady. "He's gone and frenchified it with an 'e', if you please! Pah!"

"Oh heavens!" wailed Agnes Underwood when the benches were drawn up. "I do hope the assembly will remain at table. There'll be chaos if they don't."

"I must say," said Lilian generously, "I didn't care for Mr Westcombe's sermons but he certainly had my vote on the issue of new premises."

"Unfortunately, women's votes don't count," retorted the spinster who tended to regard the wage-earning sex as a labour intensive luxury. "You'll never see any of us on the trustees committee!"

"Quite right too," interjected Tom Borderick. "A woman's place is getting the grub!"

The evening was a sensation. After tea, Mr Rodgers made a speech and formally introduced the Revd Robert Mitcheson Brown and his wife to the gathering. There followed further speeches from Bill Bradley, iron moulder, and Bob Stevenson, Lilian's better half, who welcomed the minister to what they described as an 'enlightened and progressive society' whereupon Mr Mitcheson Brown replied that he would do his utmost to further the work of God in that corner of the vineyard. "I feel a great sense of promise here," he told them. "Your labours have borne abundant fruit but there is still much to be done. If we are to gather more sheep into the fold, then the very bounds of the fold itself must be extended."

****

It was not wholly surprising that the new pastor's eloquence should not be lost upon a membership generally eager to create a good impression. If the departure of his predecessor had given rise to a few tears, it had nevertheless conferred an air of expectancy. This was obscurely comforting to Mr and Mrs Rodgers.

"That's just as it should be," she said. "The seed sown by Joe didn't germinate in his own day. Now the season's right."

John gazed out at the sky through the half-open window. The copious greenery of summer was beginning to look parched and fretted by disease. "Yes, we need that sort of perspective. It's what matters in the end."

He appeared weary beyond his years and as if the things of this world were growing tiresome, but a new light consumed his eye. "The time has come to throw down the gauntlet. The objectors must give way in the face of this latest appeal."

"A brand new chapel, think of it!"

"We must seek a plot of land. But first we need money."

Only one week later, towards the end of September, the first Quarterly Trustees Meeting of the Mitcheson Brown regime was held and inevitably the subject of larger premises was raised. It was clear that he had given the question serious consideration and was ready to go ahead with all despatch. "We must move with the times," he urged them. "This is an era of enormous change and development. History books will laud the achievements of the Empire. The church must not drag its feet."

The men of business among the group, those who had chiefly been antagonistic to further expenditure, were now in a mood to ride the tide of all that was ongoing. They certainly did not wish to be seen as an irrelevance to modern life when Methodists had gained a fearsome reputation as pioneers of both the temporal and spiritual worlds.

The chairman sighed and thanked heaven, believing his supplications had been to effect. It was a miracle of sorts. "Gentlemen, we have reached a watershed," Mr Rodgers announced.

The casting of votes proved a mere formality and in no time the meeting had set about pooling its reserves to acquire finance and a parcel of ground. They would apply for a grant. They would get up a subscription, hold entertainments, the ladies would lay on fine suppers and sales of needlework. Come the spring, they would be in a position to stake out a piece of land.

****

February came and a sleety rain fell relentlessly. The Wreake and Soar swelled fit to burst their banks. Soon the watermeadows had turned to lagoons and the cattle were confined to their stalls. After the rain, March roared in, severing brittle branches, sweeping away the debris of winter. Syston brook inched higher and higher up the arches of its bridge, as sturdy as ever after almost a century. To the residents, it seemed to have changed its whole personality, turned into a wanton tidal race, overwhelming its boundaries and rolling out through the streets.

The distress caused was in due course alleviated and such was the optimism among the Wesleyans that there were those who ventured to see in the elements an image of God's outpouring of blessing upon them. "Our meetings are full of heart and hope," reported Vincent Moore, referring to the new project. "The stream of liberality from the community is like the flood which so recently surged through our village. We have been offered donations aplenty and many promises payable within the next twelve months. Now it remains to secure a site fit for our purpose."

There were many suggestions about a possible location. Miss Elizabeth Gregory, sister of Albinia Rodgers and former schoolmistress, gave it as her opinion that the building should occupy a prominent position and should be a modern structure. She had had a thorough education and liked to attend to the nicest particulars. "Our forefathers had to build where they might, but we do not want to be lost in a backwater."

"I favour the Leicester Road," piped up Bill Bradley.

"No, by The Green," recommended Bob Stevenson. "It's where we began, out in the open."

"On the High Street," suggested Matthew Deacon, manufacturer.

The relative merits of various situations were discussed at length, but the fact remained that, as far as they knew, no ideal spot was available.

At this juncture, Black Underwood, who had been drawing quietly upon his meerschaum and keeping his own counsel, announced: "'Course, there's Tom Morris's bit o' land on High Street…"

"Next to the Bread Shop?" Bradley clarified.

Deacon, somewhat pertinently, pointed out that it had yet to come up for sale.

"He bought it off Joe Talbot and Waggy Brown nearly twenty years ago, not long after Billy Bennett died, against a rainy day," Black recalled. "Reckon he might be persuaded to sell."

"It's been derelict since I were knee-high," said Stevenson.

"Might be worth investigating," suggested the minister.

"Tom's not agin chapel folk. If we made a fair offer, I've no doubt he'd jump."

The Reverend then turned to the committee secretary. "Mr Moore, perhaps you would be kind enough to pen him a letter explaining our predicament and sound his intentions regarding the said land?"

No immediate reply came from Tom Morris which, despite a natural impatience to proceed was, on the whole, taken to be a good omen. The Sunday prayers strongly invited Divine Intervention, furtherance of the Lord's interest being, after all, their aim, and following a second approach, the shrewd speculator declared that he was prepared to enter into negotiations.

"Hallelujah!" cried the minister.

"Send Bradley and Deacon," advised Black Underwood. "They've got teeth. They'll strike a tough bargain."

The clergyman appeared wryly amused. "I'll bear that in mind, Black. I only wish John Rodgers were not indisposed. His health is a matter of grave concern to me."

"To us all," said the shoemaker. "He's a true Christian, him. There's none can follow in his footsteps."

****

It is a fact of life that, as the cobbler's own shoes are last to be mended and the lamplighter will live by the glow of a penny candle, so too the architect pays scant attention to the ramparts of his own hearth and home.

John Henry Carte's plain brick villa was no exception. To all but the keenest observer, there was nothing to distinguish it from its neighbours. It stood on Raymond Road, just off a busy thoroughfare out at Plaistow in the far reaches of the capital. South lay the Royal Victoria and Royal Albert Docks, linking Britain with the outposts of her Empire. To the west lay Whitechapel, Stepney and Bow with their rookeries, brothels and thieves' kitchens. Only last year, Jack the Ripper had cunningly eluded capture after the brutal slaughter of five prostitutes. He had been hotly pursued by the Police Commissioner himself, Sir Charles Warren, with a couple of slavering bloodhounds, Barnaby and Burgho, but the trail had been lost. The Queen was said to have gone purple with rage at the bungling ineptitude of her Force. Furthermore, the population was steadily increasing with immigrant Jews fleeing oppression in Russia and Poland. They came sailing up the Thames, tightly-packed on the boat decks, looking hunted but unvanquished, encumbered with baskets and brightly-coloured bundles. The men appeared sapient and shrunken before their time, the women and children stoical and resilient. They were never unruly - they had their own strict disciplines and it was their practice to abide by the law of the host land - but the wit with which they turned necessity to advantage aroused a good deal of antipathy.

This was the climate in which John Henry Carte had sought, by political means, to root out want and injustice. He was a young man of fierce convictions and often stormy demeanour. "We're a pragmatic movement," he would declare. "We have to use every tool at our disposal to bring about reform. We want none of your pious doling out of charity! None of your fundamentalist jam in the next world!"

His term of office as Mayor had not been entirely fulfilling, however. With the laurels some of the executive power had been lost: he had become a figurehead. He could offer no ultimate answer, but had to profess a grudging admiration of Mr William Booth's Salvation Army. They seemed to be the only religious body prepared wholesale to get their hands dirty among the lawless and destitute. And they could sing!

He paced about his library, mulling over the problem, pausing to spin the tilted globe. The spreading areas of pink paled into a giddy blur. He had just returned from Leicestershire where he had gone at his father's behest to inspect a plot of land for which the Syston chapel worthies had entered a bid. They wanted him to draw up a plan for a brave new church that would take Methodists through the next century and into the millennium! They were fairly bubbling with excitement. Mitcheson Brown had waxed lyrical about the style of elevation he favoured. Yet John Henry had felt depressed and irritated by their parochialism and their constant bleating about the fickle stocking trade. A glimpse of life in the East End and they would rapidly take stock of their blessings!

Sighing, he returned to his desk. He stared dully at the inclined plane and blank sheet before him. The redundant pencil, slide rule, compasses, protractor, had all the appearance of articles in a still life painting. But where to begin? He had administered punishment for crime. As a lay preacher, he had denounced from the pulpit the evils of strong liquor and promulgated those fine Old Testament values which had given the Victorians their prosperity. Here was his chance to use his particular skills to create something unique and lasting in the community which had nurtured him and he felt overwhelmed with defeat. Why?

What kept coming into his mind was the face of the girl in the shadows last night. She could not have been more than thirteen or fourteen - the mask of paint had not disguised that. He had missed his turning on his way back from the council chamber. The labelled streets were enveloped in fume-laden fog, stagnant with the stink of the saltmarshes and the tarry tang of vessels in harbour. His customary measured tread became halting and he had paused to mark his whereabouts by the Music Hall and the gin shop when she sprang out from the pitchblack alley. A waft of corrupt scent and something feral in the tone of her voice profoundly disturbed him. "Lost your way, 'ave you, Jamie Duff? Making haste to the grave?"

"No, of course not," he denied feebly. Under the wan gaslight, he saw how she added to the miasma by aping maturity with a long cigarillo. The tip danced like a firefly in the murky air.

"You oughta come inside for a nip o' somefing warm. Set you up nicely, that would."

"My dear child, you should be at home with your mother at this hour, minding the household."

"Ain't got no muvver. Ain't got no farver. There's just me and Archie, see? 'Ere," she said in sudden alarm, "you ain't one o' them bleedin' Peelers, are you?"

"Indeed I am not." He was unnerved by his own clumsiness and her uncouth tongue. "If I were, I might have you arrested. As it is," he said, taking out his purse and pressing a whole crown into her hand, "I'll give you this for nothing. Now take yourself off indoors and pray that God will have mercy on your immortal soul."

"Why, ain't you the toff!" she mocked, flabbergasted. "It's a quart of ale and eel pie for Archie tonight and a new titfa for me!"

He turned on his heel. "Tell me, is this the right way for the High Street?"

"Reckon it might be. You got two choices, ain't ya?"

By and by he traced his way back through the dismal night. It was chastening to realise that he had done the very thing he claimed to despise: he had dished out cold charity. He had bought her off. He had not even asked her name. Then what was he supposed to do? Lead the foul-mouthed creature home by the ear, give her a square meal and a warm bed as Mr Gladstone, the former Prime Minister, had done at some cost to his own reputation? Pray fervently that he did not contract the cholera which was rife in the area? Acquaint her there and then with the gospel? Pearls before swine, no doubt about it. But of what value was his Christianity if it could not reach out and touch those most in need? Surely no one was born past Grace.

He was sure that she had not stepped into his path by accident. The magistrate in him had been ready to rebuke her, but his faith called him not to stand in judgment. The East End streets were crawling with her kind, notoriously past reform and slippery as eels when it came to prosecution, as ready to exploit as be exploited. A slackening of trade, riots, social unrest increasing with education, the dockers striking for a pittance of sixpence an hour, all fed a subversive economy. It was a sobering fact that the modern era which was to wipe such anomalies, far from conquering evil, had merely driven it underground where it thrived as never before. And John Henry had no slick solution. Rather he began to wonder whether the buttoned-up ethics of his day, which viewed table legs as unseemly items to be swathed in petticoats, did not denote a sickened spirit. The steam age would go thundering and rolling into the unknown along predestined lines but would not alter life for the Archies of the country and their willing prey.

A tentative knock on the door signalled his wife with a pot of coffee and his favourite raisin biscuits. "A little refreshment for you, dear," she announced, noting his troubled expression. "Is anything wrong?"

Taste forbade him to speak of his encounter in the fog. "I have no appetite for this commission, Maggie. Why did I agree to it?"

Her feminine brow wrinkled becomingly. "Isn't it your chance to plough back some of what you have received?"

"But how can it signify while the people of Dockland starve, where avarice and disease abound? No one suffers in the Shires as they do here."

"Maybe not. Who can judge?"

"I have lived my life at a remove from reality. I have led a privileged existence."

"Yes, that's true. You are reaping the benefits of the faith of your father and grandfather before you. You owe them a debt."

"The world still badly needs changing."

"That is a rather tall order, dear."

"But men's hearts must first be changed. Science, learning, industrial advance, they are a means but not an end. We have taken a wrong turn."

Mrs John Henry Carte failed to suppress a tiny smile.

"Come, what is it? What amuses you so?" he demanded.

"Well" she said rashly, "men can be so blind. They begin with such passion, such nobility of purpose, and then promptly lose sight of their goal. Do you remember when you promised Ada's little sister a doll's house. Nothing would do but that it was constructed of the finest materials, an exact replica of The Queen's House at Greenwich, all done properly to scale. When that could not be obtained and you had no leisure to make one, you settled for a modest town villa, much the same as this. You said it was just the ticket!"

"That's different," he retorted pettishly. "She loved it!"

"And the Israelites of Syston will love their new tabernacle. You must not fail them, Jack. A link is a small thing but without it the chain will not hold."

He fell silent, thoughtfully stroking his moustache. She was right, of course. It was imperative to stem evil at source, to build something constructive for the glory of God where generations of his own kind might be sustained on their journey to Canaan. It was worthier to do that than to tear down icons and become embattled with the burning controversies of the day. Where there were enough healthy plants in the garden, the weeds could not flourish.

"It's where you belong, where we both belong," his wife gently reminded him.

That raddled, charcoaled face last night in the fog flashed across the screen of his mind. "I think," he said, "that somewhere betwixt there and here I have lost my way." Suddenly, he brightened. He seized his wife by the shoulders and kissed her cheek. "I perceive that the Lord made one cardinal error in giving the reins of creation to Adam. He would have been far wiser to have given them to Eve!"

"Don't refine upon it, dear. He knew how to order things!"

She reached for the doorknob and made to leave, but her husband interrupted her. "Hark! Is that music I hear?"

"It's the choir at St. Stephen's. It's the hour of their Saturday rehearsal."

John Henry craned to hear as if his very being depended upon it. "What is it? What is that they are singing?"

"Why, I believe it is 'Christ is made the Sure Foundation.'"

An hour passed. The light faded. Soon Ada, the maid from Limehouse, would creep past the door to kindle his lamp. Against a muffled chorus he had knelt and prayed for humility, that the world, even wearing its humanitarian guise, would cease to beckon. And he prayed for that nameless child, in the clutches of an unscrupulous keeper. He interceded for her body and soul and hoped that the money with which he had washed his hands of her plight would in some way be instrumental in her redemption.

Then, with the curtains drawn and the room newly aglow, he returned to the matter in hand. He thought about galleries and pillar supports, about pulpit and altar, a place for the organ and choir stalls. He thought about space and dimension and, above all, about windows. The church of the twentieth century must be filled with light!

He picked up his pencil and sharpened the stubborn graphite, then began to work with a will.

****

"They have gained the land! The site on High Street!"

John Henry let fall an exuberant letter from Mitcheson Brown regaling him with the news that the plot had been secured at a cost of one hundred and eighty pounds which was felt to be reasonable. Already they had set about calling in some of the promises and raising further funds. There was now no dearth of fresh ideas or enthusiasm for the project.

"But I knew they would do it!" cried Maggie. "When people today are so acquisitive about territory, I didn't see why the Lord shouldn't have his share!"

"They mean to begin digging by March and to have the chapel complete by harvest."

"And you have finished your plans? I hope you have not neglected them, Jack."

He grinned ruefully. "I have only to add the final touches," he assured her. "Come, I shall submit them for your approval and you can point out the errors of proportion!"

******

John Rodgers awoke to brilliant sunshine striking his brass bedstead through a gap in the dimity blinds. Quintessential light poured into the room and cancelled the disturbed hours of darkness. Mercifully, the sore, tearing pain in his abdomen had subsided to a throb after a heavy dose of white medicine and an incautious amount of laudanum.

Downstairs, he could hear a vague bustle of preparation for the luncheon party which his wife and redoubtable sister-in-law, Eliza, had risen early to undertake. This was a red-letter day in the annals of Methodism, the day appointed for the stone-laying ceremony. Joseph would arrive later, in time for the service, though his visit would be brief since Binnie had succumbed to a severe chill.

It was Easter Monday and winter had taken her foot from the door. Yesterday, they had celebrated the abandoned grave and had sung 'Thine be the Glory' with rafter-ringing gusto. The house was full of Madonna lilies and the Pre-Raphaelite indigo of early bluebells.

Yet despite the remembrance of joy, he felt uncoupled from the life around him. An April cloud passed across the face of the sun and dimmed the room to umber. He stirred, anxious to be about the business of the day, but he knew he must first wrestle with his bone-weary frame. A reviving dish of tea brought in by Albinia was a welcome sight. She flung the curtains wide, doubting that the weather would hold, for it had been too bright too early. "Oh John, you do not look equal to entertaining the President. Would you prefer a tisane?"

"I'm not an invalid yet, lass. I've had three score years and two and reckon I can manage another eight!"

But his hand did not seem quite steady, though he made a valiant attempt to control it. So she spooned in his sugar before fetching from the wardrobe the new suit Will Charlesworth, Lilian Stevenson's brother, had made for the occasion. "A fine bit of weave, that," John observed cheerfully. "Now that will outlast me!"

Three hours later, the Reverend Kelly, President of the Wesleyan Conference, and the Reverend Eldridge, Chairman of the District, joined the chapel party in the oak-beamed dining-room of Queniborough Lodge. A steaming china galleon of oxtail soup was produced, ladled ceremoniously into matching bowls and served with crisp rolls fresh from their hostess' kitchen.

"Ah," enthused Mr Kelly, "this truly is the staff of life. Believe me, without the quiet industry of your womenfolk, I am certain you could not have essayed so daring a venture."

The lady of the house blushed demurely. "It is gratifying to have such a marvellous cause, Mr President."

"That cannot be underlined enough," agreed Mitcheson Brown. "The more souls we can win, the more stable will be the life of this nation."

"Every brick in a chapel, every stone in a church," said Mr Kelly, "is a brick or stone less in a prison for England. It is ours to set the tone of public life. We must spread the news abroad to backward peoples."

The good architect's feet began shuffling uneasily under the table. "There are moments when I feel we have barely crawled out of the darkness. Our major cities are as riddled with crime and vice as ever they were. Why, the perpetrators are ten times more evil than those sentenced to penal servitude in our ancestors' day."

"All light throws a shadow," reflected John Rodgers. The voices rose and fell about him, became muted and magnified by turns.

The President of the Conference was inclined to feel that anything but a dogged optimism was a betrayal of faith. "Come, come, things have vastly improved. Let me tell you a story: A few years ago, when the Shah of Persia visited this country for the first time, he was told by the Head of the Metropolitan Police that there were four million people in London and ten thousand of them were police. "And does the Police Force keep the four million in order?" asked the Shah. 'No,' came the reply. 'Then what does?' the ruler demanded. 'Why, moral force, Your Highness,' the Chief told him."

"You will forgive me," said Carte, "if I suspect an element of propaganda in the claim. I don't see nearly enough evidence of 'moral force' as I go about the city."

"But there is a change in the wind, is there not? Men are no longer thought heroes because they can see off three bottles of port without ill effect."

Such complacency was a red rag to the ex-Mayor. "That may be so among the better-fed, but Eastenders sup their gin to deaden hunger. They cannot rely on the bounty of a rural parish where traditions of responsibility are deeply ingrained. They have learnt how to shift for themselves. They are sharp-witted and fly. Try preaching the gospel message to them!"

John Henry's wife flashed him an alarmed glance. She had rarely seen him so hot under his stiff-winged collar. "What my husband means, Mr Kelly, is that we must not neglect the mission on our own doorstep in favour of evangelism further afield."

The Guest of Honour peered over the rim of his spectacles and forced a polite little smile. "I believe I take his meaning, madam."

"We Methodists," pursued Carte, "have always prided ourselves on our practical approach to need. Time was when we rejoiced in it, but now I wonder whether in our consuming zeal to do good, we are not sliding into secularity."

"No doubt as a magistrate, sir, you have found that Acts of Parliament and systems of punishment do not make bad men good. And I would agree with you. If vice is to be driven out of the land, it will be because we are busy teaching people to love goodness, righteousness and purity. To keep the Ten Commandments and behave as men should in the sight of him who is to judge them."

"It is not enough! We must show them the Risen Christ!"

"Hear, hear," said John Rodgers under his breath.

The Reverend Eldridge, who had been noisily imbibing his soup, blotted his beard with his napkin and tried to defuse the situation by changing tack. "I fear that theology has suffered much from the ideas of Charles Darwin. I foresee a day when religion will no longer be included in general education."

"Never!" exclaimed Syston's minister. "That could never happen on these shores. We owe all our progress to it. Have our greatest reformers not been men and women of Christian conviction?"

"Well said, Robert," endorsed the President.

Once again, Carte was startled by the image of that waif in the mist. Her stark defiance still filled him with anguish. "Gifts are not always received in the spirit in which they are given," he said, a trifle obliquely. "Will the ordinary man thank God that his rights have been so earnestly defended? Will his heart remain humble? Or have we given him a stick to beat us with?"

"We can't deny," sighed Rodgers, "that education has taught folk to be discontented." He thought of days long ago when he and his grandfather had gone beating for His Grace of Devonshire's gamekeeper. The emerald dales of Derbyshire threaded with tumbledown walls and ferny clusters of larch beckoned with a kind of Elysian charm. The Duke's presence had ensured work for all. A hierarchy of servants and a network of craftsmen, farmers and those in trade had all pulled together for the common good. Everyone had a valued place in the scheme of things. There had been some poverty, but no abject want.

"The French philosopher, Rousseau, was not so wide of the mark when he claimed that probity was the daughter of ignorance," Eldridge said.

"He was misguided," the President retorted. "He had no soul for the Divine. To my mind, the idea of the noble savage is contradictory." Here he left off skimming his bowl for vestiges of meat and turned to the architect two seats from his right. "You have a valid point, Mr Carte, when you suggest that humility has been threatened. It behoves us, therefore, to teach the doctrines of the Holy Word in such a way that men will be believers and will not reject Truth because they do not know everything."

"We must walk the Emmaus Road with them," added John Rodgers, breaking bread. "Then they will know the Risen Lord."

****

It had been like hewing rock, digging out the trenches for the foundations. Nat Borderick and Joe Mason's sons had begun work when the heavy clay was in the grip of a prolonged icy spell. After the grey downpour of February, vapours lay about the valley under a silver-gilt sun to crystallise overnight in sub-zero temperatures. A glittering ghost of rime, inches thick, threw the naked trees into relief. It was awesome and magical, a cruel importer of chilblains. Nat had wielded his pick with fingerless gloves on, the better to tear out the stubborn pokeroot whose fibrous stock combined with stones as big as potatoes to slow him down. The soon familiar ring of flint on steel on the High Street was like an echo from Newby's Forge down on The Green. By the Ides of March, the frost had softened, the earth began to give way and the virgin bricks were cemented in.

"It done good, that cold snap," said Black Underwood, huddled in a threadbare greatcoat. "You was cursing like troopers when the minister's back was turned - I know 'cos I heard you - but it done the work of six men, breaking up the ground." Though not yet in his dotage, he savoured the role of elder of the tribe. He brandished his stick heavenwards. "Him Upstairs knows what he's doin' alright."

Now, with most of the congregation assembled excitedly on the site for the first ceremony of the new incarnation, he nudged John Rodgers. "I told them this was the best place for it. I knew it was right when Bradley found that tanner afore the deal was signed."

"I don't think I heard about that."

"An ancient coin, Mr Rodgers, black as the ace of spades. He rubbed it with sand to see if was one of them rare Roman jobs, but it had George III's head on and - just fancy! - the date was 1797, the year Will Cooper built our chapel. I were knee-high to a cricket when he died and don't rightly recall him, but old Mary Charlesworth, Cart as was, who passed over recently, remembered him long before he were a doddering fool like me."

Rodgers' twinkle of amusement was abruptly overtaken by a shiver. The sky had lost its morning gleam behind dark woolly cloud. Despite a cheerful countenance, he was pale and grained from the perpetual conflict with pain. He wanted nothing so much as to retire to his bed with a soothing beaker of chamomile tea.

A blustery wind buffeted the group. Skin-stinging hail began to bombard them and strew the ground with a seed pearl mantle. But they were not deterred. The Reverend Eldridge opened the service with words of triumph and Miss Underwood, striking her tuning fork against her forehead, pitched the key for the first hymn which, at the request of Mr Carte, was 'Christ is made the Sure Foundation'. Onlookers halted on the pavement nearby or stared from across the street. The blended voices carried confidently up to the Barkby Lane and down to The Green, through Chapel Street, School Street, Turn Street, Upper and Lower Church Streets, the old Goose Neck, out to the Half Croft and all the byways and backwaters of the village.

After prayers and a resounding rendition of 'Faith of our Fathers', the Guest of Honour took over. "Dearly Beloved, " Mr Kelly began, echoing the rites of matrimony, "we are gathered together in the presence of a cloud of unseen witnesses whose fidelity to the Truth in their day created the real foundation for this endeavour…"

Wrapped up against the weather, he went on to maintain that the world, though it was unaware of the fact, was riding on the backs of the faithful. Because of them, God was more inclined to deal leniently with mankind. Had he not promised Abraham that for the sake of only ten just men, judgment would be suspended on the city of Sodom?

As the sick man listened intently, a flight of doves, glowing white, ascended from the cot at Whattoffe's House and wheeled about the sky in random formation. A soft current of ecstasy poured through him and he felt lifted up above himself, the pain a separate thing now, distant, reduced. The shining side of the Easter coin was uppermost and he knew that all suffering was contained in a new order. When the moment came for him to lay the memorial stone, his shaking hand seemed guided by a power not its own. They had presented him with an ivory-handled silver trowel bearing an inscription to commemorate the event and in the cavity of the stone he placed a bottle containing copies of the *Methodist Times*, the *Methodist Recorder*, the *Leicester Wesleyan Messenger*, a list of the current trustees and a lithograph of John Henry's drawings.

Further stones were laid by a number of helpers and benefactors, including Miss Gregory who had been so ardent an advocate of the site. The strains of 'Christ, our Cornerstone' then closed the devotions, the forte markings being observed with rib-stitching fervour.

"Well, that went merry as a marriage bell," declared an elated Mitcheson Brown when they had all repaired to the Baptist Lecture Hall for tea and speeches. "The climate could hardly be said to chime with it, though!"

The gentleman from Queniborough Lodge smiled seraphically. "We were attended by angels," he said, "and William Cooper was the cheerleader."

****

The outer walls were knocked into shape during the balmier days of May and June. The cuckoo and the lark were in fine tune and, instead of hailstones, a veil of fallen blossom covered the earth. A trinity of pediments surmounted by tiny pinnacles graced the front elevation and lancet window spaces appeared on all sides. The whole was liberally dressed with honey-coloured Stanton stone which, together with the Hathern brick, came trundling across the Forest on sturdy carrier carts.

"It is just as it should be," pronounced Joseph Westcombe the moment he saw it. That day he had brought his wife down from Yorkshire to visit her parents. While the women fussed over domestic trifles, the two men were taking a stroll in the evening air. "It combines the sophistication of the modern Town Hall with a sense of spiritual sanctuary.

"Earth and ether," muttered John Rodgers.

"It is an ornament to the parish."

"You tilled the ground, Joe, and sowed the seed."

"It took the next man to nurture the growth."

"That's how it is in the great masterplan. Few live to see the best fruits of their labour."

Nathan Borderick, high on the scaffolding, beamed down at them, doffed his chequered cap and unknotted the red kerchief about his neck to wipe his brow. "Do y'hear, Mr Rodgers, sir, this'll make them Prims and Baptists look up!"

Rodgers couldn't help grinning. "And Anglicans, too, I shouldn't wonder," he said mischievously under his breath. He watched a house martin swoop under the eves of the school opposite, its small beak crammed with wattle. "We've come a long way, but we shall never cease rebuilding. As I go about this neighbourhood, visiting the sick, holding prayer meetings, sitting on committees, I'm deeply sensible of something unresolved. It grieves me that there are still factions within the wider church."

"But our persuasion was born of schism."

"Yes, we are refugees encamped in the wilderness, a travelling folk with only the dimmest memory of its origins."

"We can take care of ourselves!"

"We can, we can. And therefore we must guard against becoming too self-righteous, too detached. It is my earnest hope that one day we shall be at one with the Church of England."

"With all its meaningless cant? It's the next thing to Rome."

"Joe, lad, to hear you speak so cuts me to the quick. John Wesley loved and revered its customs, but it refused to catch his spiritual fire."

"We cannot abide empty doctrine."

"God's truth will out, nothing is surer. What have we to fear? If only those pleased to call themselves Christians were to dedicate their energies to promoting what is good, rather than combatting evil, this world might be a stonesthrow nearer heaven. But Satan likes nothing so much as to keep us preoccupied with his own awesome badness. It is what he thrives upon."

"It cannot be imagined that the Archbishop of Canterbury will be in any hurry to embrace Methodism when we ourselves are divided into two camps."

The Primitive Movement, to which Westcombe alluded, had burgeoned in Syston and moved from its pitch in School Street in 1877 to expand its activities on Leicester Road. George Handford, the learned lacemaker from Sileby, had begotten an offspring every bit as robust as William Cooper's. In his day he became President of the first Primitive Methodist Conference and was known for a powerful orator. Now, a sense of genial competition prevailed between the two chapels, but anyone with the merest perception of human nature could see how this might get out of hand. In John Rodgers' book, minds were best concentrated on mutual strengths.

"I pray that the day is not far hence when the Holy Spirit will bind us together, for I can't for the life of me see what holds us apart. Do we not cling to the self-same beliefs, sing Charles Wesley's hymns with the same gusto?"

The sun was sinking between trails of iridescent cloud, its silky warmth still hanging on the air. The older man heard as from afar the summery voices of children playing hopscotch in the dust, the broken cry of the toothless rag-and-bone man whose cart came creaking out of School Street under its weight of buckled bedsteads, weathered boots and mouldy calico. Shopkeepers brought out stiff brooms to swish the dust from their thresholds and the children shrieked with delight when the watercart came round to sluice the footpaths.

"It is for them that we toil," Rodgers said. "They are the new grain which will carry our endeavour forward."

****

It was well past midsummer when the metallic ring of the masonry hammer gave way to the plangent notes of the harmonium. The carpenter laid down his plane, the decorator his brush. Sawdust and woodshavings were swept and shovelled away and strips of wine-dark carpet spread over the varnished floorboards down the aisles.

Then the wives and the widows, the spinsters and sages, came armed with old rags, with Brasso and beeswax, to make the surfaces gleam. They brought out their chamois dipped in vinegar-water to erase fingerprints from the windowpanes, opaque and faintly tinged with mauve and sea-green. The sills and the altar were bedecked with roses, with larkspur and hollyhocks and fragrant sprigs of thyme. Next came the fringed and brocaded pulpit and altar cloths and needlepoint kneelers arranged along the rail. The tome of a Bible in a translation which no one had questioned for nearly three hundred years was opened at a passage in I Kings which described Elijah's sojourn by the brook Cherith when the ravens fed him.

At last, all was ready for the grand opening on the morrow and the whole village seemed to hold its breath in anticipation that Wednesday evening in September.

At noon the following day, they rolled out the red carpet and anchored it firmly across the chapel steps. Dr Stephenson, the revered Principal of the Children's Home was to have led the proceedings but had fallen sick, leaving the energetic Chairman of the District to step into his shoes.

"If we had bells, we would ring them!" cried Mitcheson Brown.

"Our pretty chapel is a thing of beauty and if not to be a joy for ever, at least for a very long time," opined Vincent Moore, adjusting his spectacles. A plethora of purple phrases laid siege to his mind as to how he would report the occasion in the *Wesleyan Methodist Messenger*.

Mrs Carte squeezed her husband's arm. "You did it, Jack!"

Had it not been for a foul East End mist and that wanton creature in the feather boa, he mused, I might never have got round to it. It was salutary that the Lord was quite prepared to use the fallen to gain his point with the converted!

The weather was glorious, like the Queen's Golden Jubilee three years ago. That day was still fresh as new paint in everyone's mind - there had been nothing to equal it in living memory and the revelry had gone on for a full week. Today, hearty efforts had been made to recapture its atmosphere.

A triumphal arch had been erected near the chapel and gaily coloured bunting strung up across High Street from Charles Turner's drapery at the 'top of the town' down to his brother John's grocery store by the Pinfold Wall on The Green. Half the village seemed to flock through John Henry Carte's neat Gothic portal to hear the long-rehearsed introit, *Zadok, the Priest*. Miss Underwood's choir gave a performance which owed a touch more to exuberance than to musicianship. Anthems included a piece from Mendelssohn's *Elijah* and a number of martial airs from the Sunday School. The well-turned out ranks of Eton collars, sailor suits and smocked frocks trimmed with muslin and silk were something to behold.

"That's a sight to warm the cockles of your heart," Albinia Rodgers whispered to her husband.

But though it was balm to his spirit and the fulfilment of his dreams, it was not the answer he sought. He seemed to be striving towards some other, inner revelation. Post meridian sunlight poured through the windows and gilded the swirling motes of dust which became agitated during the scuffle of hymn-singing and composed for the readings and the offering of prayer. Its mellow warmth, so different from that of the stone-laying, went through to the bone. We have travelled far since our first crude dwelling, he thought, endured many setbacks, but, throughout, our witness has not faltered. We have laid stone upon stone, brick upon brick, to arrive at this, our crowning achievement. Then why can't I enter into the fullness of joy? Perhaps my own flesh distracts me, for I am weary now.

The pain which he had managed to keep like a wolf from the door all morning, despite its distant moaning and baying, seized him in its blistering fangs so that he gripped the pew in front of him and struggled for composure. It was only through pain, through bearing the Cross, that the stones of the wilderness became the Bread of Life and the building blocks of eternity. Stones. Foundation stones. Milestones. Millstones. Whetstones. Stones removed from the path of the plough. Many was the time, in his early youth, he had tramped about the Pennine enclosures filling rush baskets with rock and pebble. All manner of stones were the touchstone of truth, but not the truth itself.

Verses of scripture pronounced in Mitcheson Brown's confident tones wove in and out of his reflections and the ebb and thrust of his agony. Earthquake, wind and fire had not marked the Lord's presence. But where was the still, small voice?

The service drew to a rousing close and every countenance he glanced upon looked happy and uplifted. Rejoicing, they surged through the vestibule and spilled out into the street, forcing brewers' drays and cabs going back and forth to the railway station to slow down. Chattering excitedly, they made their way to the Baptist Schoolroom where a 'colossal' tea awaited them. There were York hams and tongue and Melton Mowbray pork pies, Syston plum tarts, inch-thick slices of sticky malt loaf and Hovis baps from Talbott's bakery in Bath Street.

Valiantly, John Rodgers had gone ahead with his family, but when he reached the hall, he stalled in the doorway. The sight of the overladen tables with their crocheted linen, the gold-fringed curtains of ruby velvet like crushed gillyflower petals, brought out of mothballs for the occasion, and the quartet from Wyggeston School playing sprightly Gilbert and Sullivan melodies, was too much. He had neither the spirit nor the stomach for such a feast.

He laid a hand on his wife's arm. "I'll not come in to the party, lass. I fear I shan't do justice to the fare. You go with the others. Don't mind me."

"Oh my dear, the pain is troubling you again. I knew in church that it was. Let me get Hakes to drive you home."

"There's no cause for alarm. I'll not spoil the day. Just let me stroll quietly in the sunshine whilst I may."

She knew better than to persist. She let him go and prayed that God would take care of him.

The grinding pangs eased off as he turned away. With his walnut stick to lean on, he wandered down Chapel Street for a nostalgic look at the old building which had the air of a cast-off shoe. For all that, its fall from grace need not long be mourned: it would be used for many worthy endeavours within the parish. In any case, it had always appeared provisional, like a brick tent, whereas the new place had the sound authority of something planted firmly in the community.

He breathed in deep lungfuls of air which had the faint dampness of the approaching equinox. The light had a coppery gleam, he noticed, and the trees a fair scattering of ochre and rust. Youngsters were romping on The Green and tiptoeing along the low wall of the iron palisade. There, in days gone by, labourers would gather, seeking hire with the drilling and ploughing and harvesting around the valley.

Crossing to Lower Church Street, he went past the thatched cottages opposite the Wedding Door of the parish church and up through the graveyard to sit on a bench and enjoy the tranquillity. Tawny scraps of birds fluttered about, pecking at slippery yew berries. Todd's three-legged collie loped gamely down the path, bent on some errand of its own.

Sun gently drenched his skin as he leaned back against the South Wall. The chill granite struck through his Norfolk tweed. He loved the perpendicular grace of this church as he loved the rapier steeple of St. Mary's in his own parish of Queniborough and felt no betrayal in worshipping in both from time to time. Only a couple of hundred yards off stood the newly-christened chapel, a chip off the old block. A satellite.

Today had revived the excitement of Jubilee Day, but what a contrast that then all like-minded faiths had gathered to give thanks under this weathered roof and forgotten their squabbles. Such was the value of monarchy and nationhood, the unifying power of looking upward. Altar, throne and cottage, that was the natural order of things.

Seldom a whisper stirred the branches now. The air was cumbrous with crop-dust from the end of harvest and the tired pilgrim's breath grew shallower. Unsteadily, he rose to his feet and shuffled off down the side path in search of shade, his stooping, withered figure out of keeping with his years and the face he liked to present to his fellows. All these headstones, he thought, tokens of hope in the Resurrection, do not speak of comfort. The petrified cherubs, the dour vaults, the listing crosses and lichen-stained plaques emerging from unkempt tufts of grass, have nothing to do with the lives that have gone. They merely mark where the chaff has fallen on the threshing-floor.

He was drawn to Will Cooper's tomb and lingered under the awning of the copper beech. From that point he could just see the back of the chapel, the dark glitter of windows high up behind the choir stalls. His throat was dry, his head throbbed. He would go and knock on the Rectory door for a cup of water. Perhaps Tucker would let him lie down on a couch. Gazing down at the inscription on the slate, a little blurred now, something powerful quickened within him. A still small voice, an inner conviction. 'The Kingdom of Heaven is within you.'

Up above, the beech leaves were dark as blood-clots against the sky as he careened and hit the turf.

****

John Rodgers did not die that day, though he suffered a considerable haemorrhage. They found him like Elijah under the juniper tree, overwhelmed with the burden of living, next to their founder's last resting-place. He clung tenaciously to life for a further seven weeks, burning to proclaim the gospel from the new pulpit. The years seemed to have melted from his countenance and he was full of cheer. His visitors came in a steady stream to console him and be consoled themselves.

"I saw then, when I was frail and failing," he told them, "that the fabric of the temple can never be more than a symbol. In this world, the vision and the reality do not fuse into focus. But when men's hearts are right with the Maker, unity exists. That is the true Church. God be praised, it is a house not made with hands."

6

The New Grain

1897

The winter they buried John Rodgers was probably the severest of the Victorian reign and the doughty daughters of Wesley were busy stirring and simmering pans of mutton-and-turnip soup to be distributed to the fifty neediest families in Syston. The price of wheat was at an all-time low and acre upon acre of cereal land ran to grass.

It was only to be expected that a lull would follow September's apotheosis of happiness and the subsequent loss of a dearly loved member of the congregation. Then there was a vexing deficit to consider. This gave rise to a further spate of needlework sales and saw Miss Underwood's choir launched on a concert tour of chapels and village halls in the Circuit. Methodist celebrity weekends were organised and drew attendances from far afield. A connexional grant was also due and a number of donors were forthcoming to replenish the coffers. Mr John Henry Carte was one of the most benevolent. After an avalanche of support, it fell to the dauntless few to tackle the mundane problems of keeping afloat and the witness aflame. A telling piece of editorial appeared in a local Methodist journal in 1897.

'Syston alone, the queen of our villages, is stationary in its membership. Its highest and lowest records are in two successive years, 55 in 1891 and 70 in 1892. How is it that so strong a church is not stronger? Why does a Society that has so great a power *of steadfast continuance have so little power of progress? These questions deserve to engage the attention both of the Syston members themselves and of the Circuit authorities. The building of its beautiful chapel has been successfully accomplished and is evidence of the possibilities of Syston Methodism. We must pray 'that times of refreshing from the presence of the Lord' are not far distant from the place which always has been the first of our country Societies.'*

Towards the end of September, not long after the Queen had marked her Diamond Jubilee in somewhat subdued fashion, the chapel enjoyed festivities of its own, for it was a full century since William Cooper had given worshippers their first home. By now, Mitcheson Brown had moved to Lincoln but was invited to conduct the anniversary services. On the Saturday evening, John Henry delivered a fascinating talk on the history of the movement in Syston which was followed by a pork pie supper.

"We've come far since those days," reflected Paddy Stevenson, stuffing the handsome timepiece which had belonged to his grandfather back into his waistcoat pocket, "though the price of a loaf is higher than ever."

"We have been the prime movers in gaining a better deal for the working man," boasted Mitcheson Brown.

"We have doled out food to the hungry," added Charles Mason, spearing some of the pickled walnuts his grocery chain had supplied.

John Cart guided his shaky fork to his mouth. Lately he appeared to have retreated into his shrunken fame and the joints of his fingers were knobbed with arthritis. "Today we give out of our abundance where once we gave out of our want," he said hoarsely. "Time was when many of our friends were ashamed to own us because of our beliefs."

William Bradfield, the minister, blotted his lips with a napkin. "Indeed, indeed. Much has been achieved but something holds us back."

"Holds us back, sir!" cried his predecessor. "How can you say so?"

"I was thinking of that article I showed you earlier."

"Is the Kingdom of God to be measured by attendance at service?"

"It is a barometer, surely." Leaning forward, Mr Bradfield appealed to a good-looking fellow with a face as brown as tea leaves seated further along the table. "What is your opinion, Walter? You have seen a fair bit of the world."

Whilst his brother, William James, had remained in Syston to assume the responsibilities of the family tailoring business, Walter Charlesworth had spent the past eleven years in the Ceylon mission field where he had gone after studying for the ministry at Richmond College. Now he was on furlough and his impression of English values was fuelling the conviction that his life might be spent as profitably on home soil. At the time of his going abroad, the seed of the plan for a larger chapel had barely germinated. Now, although there was sturdy growth, there was also a sense of resting on laurels. Ironically, he found he had an ally in its architect who might have been expected to glory in the material rather than the mystical.

Walter pictured the tin shacks and shanty towns of Ceylon, the little wooden mission hut packed to bursting, the fierce skies and bold, frond-like vegetation, the languid stretches of paddy field which kept its ebony-eyed natives occupied from daylight to dark. It was impossible to convey the tenor of life there which ruled out most of the getting and having peopled took for granted in Britain. Walter's smile was inscrutable and his voice soft as he fixed his listeners with eyes that were zircon-bright against his tanned skin. "I sense a dreadful darkness looming over the West," he said. "There is an overweening desire to conquer and acquire which distorts the natural simplicity of the gospels. They say that Jesus Christ was a carpenter by trade, but more than that, he was the perfect husbandman. What's planted in faith can't fail to yield a harvest."

"You are right!" exclaimed Mr Bradfield, as though his course had been determined. "Our church has become too much preoccupied with the outward and visible."

"John Rodgers, 'rest his soul, used to say that," reminisced Cart senior. "He was truly a prophet among us and there has been no one to fill his shoes."

It was then that Walter resolved to return to Britain as soon as he had fulfilled his obligations in the East.

****

Just before Burns night, 1901, the frail old Empress shuddered, sighed, and was gone. She had ailed for many weeks following a punishing round that would have taxed a Sovereign half her age. At Christmas she retired to Osborne House on the Isle of Wight to convalesce and the slackened pace proved too great a shock for a frame accustomed to seamless activity.

No sooner had the tiny coffin made its stately journey to the mausoleum at Frogmore, than Miss Underwood got out the score of Stainer's *Crucifixion* which she proposed to rehearse with the choir during the season of Lent. Her proper feelings of sadness at bidding farewell to the Victorian rule were tinged with a sneaking sense of liberation. The old regime had grown stale and outmoded. And a coronation would be fun.

King Edward, it had to be said, was a fine figure of a man with an air of authority and an endearing penchant for the ladies. He loved pomp and display and believed in making a bright spectacle of royal traditions. There were those who claimed he was nowhere near as politically astute as his mother had been, but he did have wit and charm. The sight of him stiffened the nation's pride in its achievements and reminded those abroad that Britain was Great.

Yes, for all her awareness of the shortcomings of the male, Miss Underwood thought that things were changing for the better. There had been no man in her life apart from her shoemaker father and no one could hold a candle to him. She had cared for him until his death and was now firmly wedded to her music and her school teaching. In any case, eligible men were a scarcity these days. They had forsaken the homeland in droves and were scattered far and wide in the cause of the Empire. Then there was the war in South Africa which had sparked and flared for ever, it seemed, because the arrogant Dutch were robbing the Cape of its mineral resources and did not know how to treat the natives. Left to fend for themselves, women had grown bold and resourceful. They had begun to chafe under the yoke of centuries and demand new freedoms. They had gained rights to their own property and could no longer be legally detained at home by their husbands.

Now, the future crackled with expectancy. "Fling wide the gates! Fling wide the gates!" warbled Miss Underwood as she scuttled off to the larder, pungent with strings of onions and John Turner's best 'mousetrap' cheese. There she sliced a neat doorstep of bread, spread it thickly with dripping and poured a celebratory nip of elderberry wine. Each autumn she could be spotted along the byways and hedgerows, her arm looped through a basket, snipping pendulous clusters of fruit with a pair of embroidery scissors. She enjoyed fussing over her preserves, loved to see the crimson and garnet colours paraded along her shelves, the captured mellowness of Syston Whites glistening with syrup. It was a shame, she felt, not to try her hand at homemade wine merely because she had signed the pledge. After all, the true meaning of temperance was not abstinence. And since neither vinery nor vintner had profited from her guilty little secret, she did not think it could be counted a sin. Smart modern women were growing fond of a drop of liquor. They had started aping men and wearing knickerbockers so that they could ride unimpeded on their penny-farthing bicycles. Miss Underwood fancied herself upon such an instrument. She could ride around the lanes to her heart's content, scattering hens and geese, the dust flying behind her. When she voiced such an ambition to George Preston, the Postmaster, mainly because she delighted in provoking him, he told her that women and machines went ill together. She'd either break her neck or fall foul of a molester. The latter, he admitted to himself, seemed the less likely of the two!

"Stuff and nonsense!" she retorted through the grille. "No use looking for shelter and protection when our men have fled to faraway spice islands and the South African veldt."

Mr Preston detached a strip of postage stamps from the page of multi-profiled King's heads. "They're doing their duty. They're defending you and your heritage."

"At arm's length! While they're running off to sow plantations and create mayhem and massacre abroad, we are left to run the country."

"They always did say: the hand that rocks the cradle...!" said the Postmaster in ironic tones. But Miss Underwood ignored him.

"It is not what God intended, Mr Preston," she stated categorically. "However, we must get on with it. We have no choice. You'll see, it won't be long before women take their rightful place in Parliament!"

"And in the pulpit too, I shouldn't wonder," he mumbled as she flounced out of the door.

****

Mercifully, the peace treaty signed at Vereeniging during May of the following year drew the final curtain on the Boer War.

In the village, to mark the relief of Mafeking, they set a torch to a massive bonfire on Riley's cricket field. Mounted upon it was a scarecrow effigy of Kruger. The children clapped and jumped around with glee when the seat of his breeches smouldered, then burst into a crackling rush of flame and glinting wisps of ash.

****

That Leicester was one of the first towns in England to have a museum and the last to organise a lending library, speaks of conflicting forces behind its public face. It seemed unable to let go the past.

Nowhere was this more strongly in evidence than upon the issue of education. Even the museum building, designed by Joseph Hansom who is remembered more for his cabs than his architecture, had set out as the Proprietory School but had fallen on hard times.

Reformers of differing creeds had vied with each other during the Victorian era to found schools, but standards were inconsistent and such teaching failed to reach those most in need. The Board Schools of 1870 had gone some way to advancing primary instruction, but attendance was not compulsory. Children were still needed for the economy of the workplace and arrived for part-time lessons too tired to spell or count.

By the turn of the century, Balfour's administration was determined to crack the problem. A state system of secondary education was introduced with strict laws against absence. Both voluntary and Board Schools would be equally accountable for good standards. In return for the use of the former's premises, certain expenses were to be met out of the rates.

There followed an unholy furore. Nonconformist Liberals who had gained the ascendancy since the days of the machine-breakers and who could be relied upon to champion the deprived, did not welcome this wholesale approach. They jibbed at paying rates to support the infant Anglican and Roman Catholic alongside the Baptist, Quaker or Methodist.

"It is scandalous! Quite scandalous!" Agnes Underwood declared. She raised flinty eyes from her local broadsheet and peered over the top of metal-rimmed spectacles at Cooper, the marmalade feline who had roundly settled himself on the tablecloth. "The Church of England has always existed for those who are plump in the pocket. We Dissenters have been responsible for lifting up the heads of the poor and we are called upon to carry *them*!"

Cooper, utterly unmoved by this tirade, sized up the creamer, the snowy tip of his tail twitching smugly. He was sharp enough to understand that in the light of such anomalies, his own depredations would go unnoticed.

His mistress aired her views in shops and sitting-rooms and, though she found argument stimulating, was pleased that the consensus of opinion was with her. When the Reverend Allan Holt rashly suggested that Christians ought to be above political controversy, she countered that if he thought that, he ought not to be a Methodist! God needed them to be a thorn in the flesh of all who tolerated inequality.

"Come now, Agnes," he said soothingly, "nothing could be more egalitarian than this latest Act of Parliament. It has courage, integrity and vision."

"It is unashamed fraud!"

"Children of the poor will be taught in established schools. Think what new buildings would cost the ratepayer."

"The burghers of Leicester do not share your view, Mr Holt. They and their fathers and grandfathers before them have fought for the rights of common people. Some of them are prepared to be jailed for their principles."

"They must do as conscience dictates. As I see it, there is something perverse in the notion that this is a divisive measure. It is the greatest stride yet towards true democracy."

"If that is so, why is Mr Sawday himself refusing to pay his taxes?"

Leicester's Lord Mayor, Albert Edwin Sawday, was an architect colleague of John Henry Carte and sometimes attended worship at Syston's High Street chapel. After he had relinquished his chains of office, he was to join the committee of trustees.

The storm died down and the first generation of Britain's young sat down together to gaze at blackboards and recite Psalms and tables, parrot-fashion.

Miss Underwood continued to teach in the village but several years later was obliged to retire as chapel organist and choir mistress owing to sprained tendons in her fingers and a stiffness of the spine. The imposing instrument which had been installed since the early days was too demanding for her frame. Her years of service, which had seen some notable and historic moments, were much appreciated and she was presented with a silver key to the organ and a generous cheque. For once, she stumbled over words of thanks and said she hoped that Mr Neston, her successor, would have many more occasions to pull out all the stops.

****

The dizzy Edwardian era was brief. All too soon the enchantment blazed and faded like a spent firework.

Edward Albert had come to his mother's throne late in life and had packed his decade of power with as much festivity as it was possible to savour. His splendid balls and banquets, at which he played host to the luminaries of every nation, were designed to show off the trophies of victory and to recommend him as the world's leading light. This drove his nephew, Kaiser William of Germany, insane with envy. He was convinced that his own country was the superior race. Had it not galloped ahead since the union of its provinces? At the same time, it had lost out to its neighbours in the race to acquire colonies abroad and lay claim to large tracts of the earth's surface. Now it could only look eastward to the Balkans as a means of creating an empire of its own.

Almost overnight, the shrinking globe was thrown into a ferment. Events jostled for the headlines. Scott followed Amundsen to the South Pole. Sopwith was circling over Windsor Castle - Bleriot had already flown across the Channel - and the ill-fated Titanic went down, despite being a remarkable feat of engineering. Suffragettes paced up and down Piccadilly demanding votes for women or else tied themselves to the railings of 10, Downing Street. After the great rail strike, there was a coal strike. The feuding Irish screamed for Home Rule. War broke out in the Balkans. German Dreadnoughts slid one after another into the sinister waters of the new Kiel Canal for surveillance of the Baltic and North Seas. *'Der Tag'* was the toast of their seamen, when the English and the French were to be subdued.

It was as though all the evil in the world had become clearly focused. Newspapers gave off a vague air of menace. Billboards alerted commuters to events which appeared to have little to do with their daily transactions. Places with strange-sounding names like Bosnia, Herzegovina and Sarajevo, which might have been culled from some legend or fable, were murmured up and down the land.

The Reverend Waverley and his band at Syston worked hard to fund renovations to the chapel which was now over twenty years old and had come into its wants. The trustees were calling for electric lighting to be installed. Talks were given on such subjects as 'Hindrances to Good Citizenship' and there were lantern lectures featuring the North Pole and The Alps. Miss Lottie Nourish, renowned locally for her mellow contralto voice, gave recitals, and the choir, under the exacting baton of Mr Edwards, continued to give performances around the Circuit.

Then, all at once, the past and the future were riven asunder. The Bosnian peasant and crackshot, Gavrilo Princep, took aim at Ferdinand, powerful Archduke of Austria, and a whole way of life bit the dust.

In August 1914, Britain went to war with her German cousins.

****

And now, as winter encroached, they forsook their homefires, the men of Wreake, to defend their liberty against forces they had not dreamt of. It was not only distance and mortal danger which separated them from loved ones. It was altered horizons.

"It's Alfred Preston at the Post Office I don't envy," said John Turner coming down from the stepladder he had used to stack a display of tinned Ovaltine. "Not a pleasant job when you've to deliver telegrams to the bereaved."

Old Will Charlesworth, doddery but stoutly shunning a walking-stick, had shuffled into the shop for a couple of ounces of the special blend of tobacco he favoured. The interior smelled of smoked hams which were veiled in muslin and hooked on a low beam, roast coffee, Brasso and Sunlight soap. He looked a trifle bewildered as he brushed a veteran's hand over his pale silver stubble and tried to formulate the right sentences.

"Had to come," he said. "World's gone too far down the primrose path. Over by Christmas, they say... anything could happen... Asquith's bunch in the driving-seat."

"Never mind, Granddad," Turner teased, wrapping the shag in a twist of greaseproof paper and winking at the next customer, "with this in your pipe, you can forget your troubles. They'll not be conscriptin' you in a hurry."

The formidable strife abroad forced communities at home to bond together. In Syston, Dr Dalley from The Gables at the 'top of the town' was rushed off his feet prescribing for an epidemic of Spanish 'Flu which seemed as grim a reaper as the war itself. Nevertheless, villagers enjoyed a thriving social life, none more so than the Wesleyans. Will Charlesworth's young relative, Leslie Simpson, was enlisted to help Superintend the Sunday School and Mr and Mrs Benjamin O'Vastar, a sparky Irish couple, held class meetings for a pack of lively young people. Miss Mason, whose ancestor was John Tookey, one of the earliest trustees of the chapel, held a gymnasium group for girls in the old premises and, in summer, coached them in tennis on Farmer Fox's court in Turn Street.

An end to fighting brought effervescent relief and the style of life characterising the twenties. Food supplies were thinly stretched as the rusty wheels of commerce ground into motion. The Co-operative Movement, which began in the north and had spread as far south as The Midlands, was a boon to many a family budget. On 'divi' day, children were let out of school early to collect their dues. Meanwhile, the steely men of Jarrow trudged the blistering, bone-sore miles to Downing Street to beg for work. It was an outrage that those who had been ready to submit to the firing line for their country had no bread. Respect for authority was fast diminishing.

Miss Underwood, well-advanced in years but amazingly sprier than she had been earlier, was in transports of delight when women of twenty-one were granted the vote. She was of the fixed opinion that the civilising influence of the female would do much to usher in the millennial reign. While men were barbaric and bone-headed enough to go to war, no Messiah would wish to dwell among them. "I don't know what the world is coming to," she lamented, counting cash in the minister's vestry one Sunday. "Look what a débâcle men have made of things! Whatever happened to decency and honour and common humanity?"

The visiting lay preacher, a man of some wisdom and considerable grace, studied her for a moment before lifting his coat off its peg. "They are, as ever, for those who have ears to hear and eyes to see."

"That is all very well," she returned impatiently, "but society does not listen to the Church nowadays."

"I doubt it ever paid much more than lip-service, Miss Underwood. Events have merely forced it to show its hand. But, thanks be to God, our number is swelling. We are the leaven of the whole batch. Ours is a silent revolution."

****

They said it couldn't happen twice. Barely were the children of the Armistice raised when Europe trembled again on the brink of World War. Two decades of memorials faithfully incarnadined with poppies each November and the slaughter of the Somme, Passchendaele and Ypres had done nothing to restrain the powers bent on combat.

In Germany, the scions of royal courts no longer held sway. A fanatical Führer had arisen to appeal to the nation's martial streak and polarise its will for supremacy.

Walter Charlesworth, now an elderly supernumerary but still possessed of the prescient blue eyes of youth, read his newspaper with growing dismay. "It is the conceit of Lucifer himself," he said darkly.

Leslie Simpson frowned. "It's for the youngsters that I mind so much. We teach them to make peace, that the tyrant shall not prevail, and yet here we are, less than a generation from the greatest haemorrhage of history, and what have we learned? No one will persuade me that it is the will of God."

"My friend, if the human ego, the Adam in every person, does not die for a God of love and compassion, then the price must be paid in the flesh."

****

But every cloud has a silver lining and every crucible its gold. With their usual sangfroid, the people of the Wreake Valley came into their own. Blackouts, gas masks, coupons, an influx of soldiers billeted without warning upon their homes, saw their humour high and the denominations working together. As never before, they flocked into their churches to pray for deliverance and for the safe-keeping of loved ones far afield. Each Wednesday evening, at the High Street chapel, the Reverend Ward led a prayer meeting and mentioned by name the servicemen from the Wesleyan family. On the eve of Dunkirk, the Sunday School celebrated its fortieth 'sermons' to be held in the building and sang like larks in a meadow.

"I am fully determined that the devil shall not win," announced Mr Ward from the pulpit. "We have a gospel to proclaim…"

"A heritage to cherish," said Walter Charlesworth later. "I suspect that William Cooper would be well pleased that his chapel is being used as a Civil Defence Headquarters in times such as these."

"And there are new foundations to lay," added Leslie Simpson. "When Mr Carte passed away last year, he left this village one of its greatest legacies. We must see that our small charges carry on the tradition and pray for the time when our schoolrooms are full to overflowing so that their children must seek expansion. Can we hope for a happier testimony than that?"

As the war dragged on, Mr Ward's ministry gave way to Mr Sheldon's. No sooner had he become familiar with the affairs of the Circuit than he realised the unusual potential of the church to which he had been assigned. He made sure that he wrote to every soldier whose family was represented in his congregation and sent postal orders from the 'comforts' fund he had instituted.

After the war, he was inspired to write a brief chronicle of the path these hardy Nonconformists had trodden which was delivered with brio on the one hundred and fiftieth anniversary of the first chapel.

Ten years later, following prolonged intercession and the patient diplomacy of the Reverend Henry Hollman, the Primitives and Wesleyans of Syston joined permanently for worship in John Henry Carte's church. Twenty-eight years had elapsed since the Deed of Union making provision for such an event.

Nearly two centuries of witness to the same Lord had brought them together and it was understood that Methodists in the village numbered twice the national average per head of population.

It was, as Mr Hollman remarked, a marriage made in heaven.

7

The New Crop?

1987

They have passed away now, the old school. They have become dust and ashes. What lives on is their psyche to fire the present generation. Through its Home and Overseas Missions, Methodism has cast its net over the whole planet. Members of the Junior Missionary Association post pennies of pocket money into their coin-box globes, confident that their prayers and practical help will not go amiss.

The Sunday School at Syston prospered and got its new home, a large suite of rooms designed by Mr Allen of Wanlip and completed free of debt. The Hall was dedicated by the Reverend Oliver Phillipson, general secretary of the Department of Chapel Affairs and opened by the beloved Superintendent of the Leicester North Circuit, the Reverend Arthur Bland in June, 1965.

During the seventies, Michael Chester, who had taken on the ministerial mantle at Syston, used the premises to mount an exhibition of the area's Methodist heritage, for it was two hundred years since William Cooper had purchased the plot of land in Town Street as part of the Whattoffe's House estate.

Michael made a pilgrimage to Epworth, the Lincolnshire rectory where John Wesley had grown up, perhaps where the first seeds of departure from orthodoxy had been sown, and realised that the founder's faith was still vibrantly alive. Wesley had been the rebel chosen to stem an English revolution. 'A brand plucked from the burning' was how he described his dramatic rescue from the flames which consumed his boyhood home. Not for nothing had he and his disciples been dubbed 'Methodists'. They had adapted to changing circumstances, construed the living gospel of Jesus Christ according to the dynamics of their time. There were those who complained that Wesley would turn in his grave if he knew the modern church's stance on some of the controversial issues of the day. But Michael would politely disabuse them. "No," he would say, "you are mistaken. It is exactly what the Great Man would have wanted!"

By the time his successor, Martin Smithson, had prepared the ground for his ministry, there was a growing awareness that the hundredth birthday of the High Street chapel would fall during his period of service and a sense of privilege and excitement began to take hold of him. Three years in advance, a committee was formed to raise funds and organise convivial events. One of its members, Frances Lewis, a keen and accomplished photographer, hoped that some of her pictures might be used in the proposed booklet of the chapel's history.

It was a cool autumn day, cloudy-bright and damp when Martin drew up on the gentle ascent in Turn Street to enjoy a cup of tea and a slice of cherry cake in the parlour of her little cottage. He had just driven across The Ridgemere from South Croxton. The air was pungent with woodsmoke, the withered prunings and rotten vegetation of summer cremated in the bonfire's cleansing flame. In the denuded fields, the plough, besieged by a flock of raucous gulls, steadily churned over the red-brown clay ready for a planting of winter wheat.

Miss Lewis was at pains to enlarge the young clergyman's knowledge of the district's past and fetched out a stack of albums, old journals, dog-eared and faded cuttings.

"Our founder was a humble farmer," she explained. "A son of the soil."

"What better?" smiled Martin, thinking of the gospels teeming with images of husbandry. "The Parables are all about sowing and reaping and tilling the land." The world has become so complex and sophisticated, he thought, hoist with the petard of its own ingenuity. After two global conflicts and the shadow of a nuclear holocaust, it is hard for human beings to believe in any cause, let alone a God. "It is a pity we've lost our affinity with the earth," he said.

"Alas, that simple faith vanished long ago."

"And yet, you know, it is still an imperative. We must be like trusting infants to be fit for the Kingdom and that's why we shall make them the focus of attention during our celebrations. The children of our church family are not only the church of tomorrow, they are the church of today."

When he took his leave, she saw him across the threshold and called to him as he unlocked his car door. "Remember, there's no way out ahead. This used to be called Turn Again Street."

Turn Again Street. The phrase seemed to have the ring of a commandment as Martin engaged the gears and drove off.

****

The high water mark of the centenary is long over. The committee has disbanded. The target sum of twenty thousand pounds needed to overhaul the heating system, build a ramp for the very young in pushchairs, the elderly and disabled, and undertake other repairs has been exceeded. It was a year of great rejoicing, of pulling together, of reaching out to the wider community.

There was a Civic Service shared with other denominations, a series of concerts, a pantomime and an 1890's Music Hall, garden fêtes and barbecues, an auction of talents in which the bold and the generous put up their free time and their capabilities for sale. One hundred and twenty-seven children enjoyed a mammoth tea party in the Hall and were afterwards entertained by Jimbo, the magician. Sunday worship was conducted by a string of illustrious personalities, among them the Revd Bryan Hindmarsh, Vice President of the Methodist Conference. Chairman of the Oxford and Leicester District, the Revd Edward Lacy, officiated at the centenary of the stone-laying. Those present included relatives of Mr Leslie Charlesworth Simpson and Mr and Mrs David Rodgers whose ancestor had himself been such a cornerstone of

Wesleyanism in the valley.

It was Mrs Dorothy Palmer, granddaughter of William James Charlesworth, tailor, who proudly unveiled a plaque to commemorate the occasion and was keenly conscious of forging a new link in a long chain of witness.

****

Martin Smithson's day at Syston is drawing to a close. He will be moving on shortly to break new ground. The paraphernalia of everyday life is being stowed in cardboard boxes. Both he and Judith share their three children's sadness and elation. Their sojourn has been one of immense blessing and adventure. They have explored the very roots of the faith they cherish and are encouraged to know that Syston Methodist Church has been singled out as the one in the Circuit with the greatest potential for growth. During his ministry, Syston has attained town status with a rapidly expanding population in the teens of thousands. For the foreseeable future, perhaps into the millennium, Mr Rogers, the new incumbent, will inherit the field to harvest and sow as seems best to him.

Martin sits at his desk, toying with a pencil, and gazes out at the unkempt roses creeping over the windowsill, wondering what message of hope in these troubled times he will leave with the friends here. Social chaos is every bit as acute as it was in previous eras. Poverty remains unchecked: there are those who claim that food is scarcer for some than in the workhouses of their great-grandfathers. Anarchy erupts on the streets and the mask of civilisation is cracking. The desperate pour scorn upon believers and the poor still find that they misfit the pew. Church unity takes laboured steps and the issue of women priests has split the Establishment in two.

Maybe Martin's hope is best summed up in the advice and the promise from the Sermon on the Mount. 'Seek first the Kingdom and the rest shall be added.' It is as profound and old as the hills and as new as tomorrow's dawn.

Suddenly, his head is filled with echoes from the past. "Plough a straight furrow, lad. Fix your eye on the far side and never look back."

The still, small voice fades…and is gone.

www.ingramcontent.com/pod-product-compliance
Lightning Source LLC
Chambersburg PA
CBHW071516040426
42444CB00008B/1676